BOOK OF GADGETS AND INVENTIONS

Robb Pearlman

Running Press

PHILADELPHIA

Running Press
Hachette Book Group
1290 Avenue of the Americas, New York, NY 10104
www.runningpress.com
@Running_Press

Printed in China

First Edition: October 2019

Published by Running Press, an imprint of Perseus Books, LLC, a subsidiary of Hachette Book Group,
Inc. The Running Press name and logo is a trademark of the Hachette Book Group.

The Hachette Speakers Bureau provides a wide range of authors for speaking events.
To find out more, go to www.hachettespeakersbureau.com or call (866) 376-6591.

The publisher is not responsible for websites (or their content) that are not owned by the publisher.

Print book cover and interior design by Rachel Peckman.

Library of Congress Control Number: 2019939200

ISBNs: 978-0-7624-9435-4 (flexi-bind), 978-0-7624-9433-0 (ebook)

RRD-S

10 9 8 7 6 5 4 3 2 1

CONTENTS

INTRODUCTION

"Science, huh? Ain't it a thing."

—Morty

Welcome to the world of *Rick and Morty*! Though I suppose it would be more accurate to say, thanks to portal guns and other technology, the *worlds* of *Rick and Morty*. I think we can all agree that without the fantastic gadgets and inventions featured in Dan Harmon and Justin Roiland's hit show, *Rick and Morty* would be nothing more than a standard basic cable sitcom about a dysfunctional suburban family and the wacky hijinks that ensue when their alcoholic, sociopathic, narcissistic patriarch comes to live with them. Yeah, that old trope. Again. Lucky for us, rather than "very special episodes" in which lessons are learned and hugs are shared in under 30 minutes, we get *science*. More importantly we get Rick's depraved manipulation of science that provides audiences across multiple planes of reality with a nonstop, cross-dimensional adventures filled with clones, deep state conspiracies, sex robots, and, of course, a few laughs along the way.

Rather than having to wait for the temporary superintelligence that comes as a side effect of mega seeds dissolving in your rectal cavity, let this book teach you all about some of the best tools and devices that exist, in our reality at least, in *Rick and Morty*'s first three seasons.

BODY & MIND

As PSAs have shown us in graphic and metaphoric detail, the human brain can look and behave very differently when substances and technology are directly applied to it. For example, if it's cracked open and fried in a pan over high heat, it will look more like the focal point of a tasty brunch dish rather than a gelatinous pink walnut.

There's nothing that's more invasive, revolutionary, and potentially godlike than technology that directly affects and augments a living being. Whether it's intended to raise intelligence or modify a body, the inventions created by Rick Sanchez earn his place alongside Prometheus, Frankenstein, or whoever it was that invented underwear that makes butts look bigger.

That's flattering and a little weird.

Do you have any concept of how much higher the stakes get out there, Morty?

Jeez, Rick, I was just trying to say something nice.

Yeah, I saw that.

ANATOMY PARK

An entire miniature amusement park found inside Rick's old friend Ruben, who fell upon hard times shortly after the dot com crash in the early '90s, Anatomy Park features some of the best attractions you've never seen. Created by Rick and his friend Dr. Xenon Bloom to earn some money to offset the extraordinary costs associated with science, Anatomy Park is, first and foremost, a living museum of humanity's most noble and most ferocious diseases, including the dreaded Hepatitis A and Hepatitis C, tuberculosis, gonorrhea, bubonic plague, and, of course, E. coli. But because those diseases are highly prized by those who would like to decimate the population (including Al-Qaeda, North Korea, balding men that work out, and people on the Internet that are only turned on by cartoons of Japanese teenagers), the park is subject to sabotage.

Who is such a good guy.

Despite the threat, families can spend days enjoying Spleen Mountain, Bladder Falls, Pirates of the Pancreas (located in Lower Abdomenland), the Cerebral Cortex Carousel, the Haunted Liver, Colon Log Ride, and the Lung Lift-Off. Safety is of moderate concern, so hold on to the handrails during your trip on the Arterial Transit System. In case of emergency, you should take the service shuttle connected to the skeletal system, also known as the Bone Train. *The Bone Train.*

Unless you're a microbe, you will need to wear some sort of apparatus to help you breathe, especially if the body

That's my baby.

you're in is dead and filling with gas. But though the helmet and tank may look unwieldy, they're surprising light and will not impede your enjoyment of the rides, attractions, or food courts. Should you find yourself in any gastrointestinal danger after a full day's worth of fun, the Sphincter Dam, originally built to help Ruben with his perpetual incontinence, has enough structural integrity to withstand the most egregious of any living organism's dumps.

First Appearance: Season 1, Episode 3: "Anatomy Park"

Seriously, do yourself a favor and pop by Pirates of the Pancreas . . . I think it's great. It's a bunch of pirates running around a pancreas. We don't whitewash it either . . . the pirates are really rapey. You gotta go treat yourself.

ANIMAL TRANSLATOR

Using sonar technology and the same base mechanics as Rick's universal translator, the device sits on your head like a pair of overdesigned, superexpensive headphones. However, instead of being constructed out of a cheap set of wires made in an Asian sweatshop and then wrapped in trendy plastic and leather to be pawned off on the masses of social media zombies, the animal translator consists of three radio telescopes that pick up and automatically translate the verbal and nonverbal words of animals.

First Appearance: Season 3, Episode 8: "Morty's Mind Blowers"

ANTI-PICKLE SERUM

As any home chef knows, the best way to counteract saltiness is to dilute and absorb, thus, an anti-pickle serum may be concocted. Using distilled water, radioactive iodine, and pureed potatoes —which, in addition to absorbing the salt, adds significant amounts of potassium, creating potassium iodine—you can create a solution which further counteracts the radioactive pickling.

This is just sloppy craftsmanship.

As a pickle, you may find it difficult to return to your original form. Plan to place a syringe filled with the fluid hanging directly over yourself, with a string attached to it running through a pair of scissors attached to a timer set to 10 minutes from whenever your family would have left for therapy.

First Appearance: Season 3, Episode 3: "Pickle Rick"

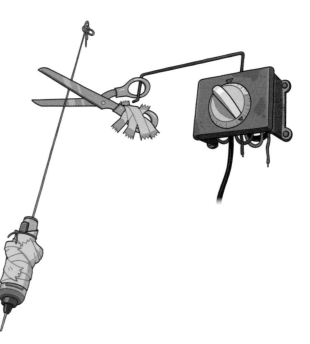

"Come on, flip the pickle, Morty. You're not going to regret it. The payoff is huge."

—Rick

COGNITION HELMET

Snuffles didn't mean it, he is a good dog.

With the ability to tap into the brain without penetrating the skull, the cognition helmet fits comfortably on any canine's cranium. Initially conceived as a crazy science thing that could make Snuffles, the Smith family dog, smarter, the cognition helmet belies the very purpose of having a dog: to feel superior. It uses a series of electrodes centered particularly above the auditory and speech centers, and is connected to a speech device that converts thought to sound. Similarly, the helmet features a concentration of sensors located directly above and around the cerebellum, which gives the wearer the ability to transfer the thought of movement to any robotic or supplemental appliance in its network. *or A stupid Jerry*

But as science, and <u>fate</u>, would have it, when you give a dog a cognition helmet, he's going to become self-aware. And when he becomes self-aware, he's going to notice the small access point on the front of the helmet. And when he notices the access point, he'll open it and begin to probe the internal circuitry.

And when he probes the circuitry, he's going to figure out how to boost the connections leading into his cerebellum. And when his cerebellum is boosted, he'll build a more advanced machine that not only gives him a prehensile claw perfect for changing the channels on a remote control or hard wiring complex robotics, but also a speech device. And when he gains the ability talk, he's going to ask serious questions about where his testicles are.

And when he learns what has happened to his testicles, he's probably going to need to chill out and watch television. And when he watches television, he'll learn about humanity's cruel subjugation of his species and form an all-dog army outfitted in robotic exoskeletons to turn the tables and make dogs, not man, the preeminent species on Earth.

So don't give a dog a cognition helmet and just let him pee on the rug.

First Appearance: Season 1, Episode 2: "Lawnmower Dog"

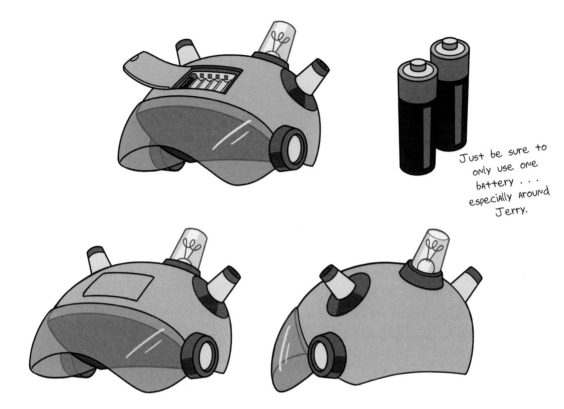

Just be sure to only use one battery . . . especially around Jerry.

"You can't endow a creature with sentience and then take it away."
—Summer

CRONENBERG SERUM

Created as an antidote to the mantis serum, which was in turn an antidote to the vole oxytocin. It combines a mixture of:

- koala
- rattlesnake
- chimpanzee
- cactus
- shark
- golden retriever
- and just a smidge of dinosaur chemicals

This serum is so powerful that the rate of contagion is capable of infecting the world's population (except those with the same DNA as the initial host) at an alarming rate. Those affected are turned not into benignly flirty or malignantly stalkery paramours, but into horrific amalgamations of never-before-seen surrealist monsters that can only be described as Cronenbergs.

First Appearance: Season 1, Episode 6: "Rick Potion #9"

Rick Fact

"Cronenbergs" are named after famed film director and writer, David Cronenberg. Despite being born in Canada—perhaps the cleanest, most polite country on Earth in any dimension—he made his name in the cesspool that is Hollywood, USA, for his provocative, imaginative, and oftentimes visually graphic films including 1981's *Scanners* and 1986's *The Fly*.

Look at this guy, thinking that by dropping bits of Hollywood trivia Tinsletown will take notice and option the screenplay he's been writing for the past seven years in coffee shops around the country. Good luck with that, pal.

DREAM INCEPTOR

Rooted in the science of everyone's favorite movie that really doesn't make sense, the dream inceptor is a device that, when put in your ear, lets you enter people's dreams.

See, Rick? He said "favorite."

Okay, Morty, like you really should trust this guy's opinion on anything.

All you have to do is insert the earpiece into all of the dreamers' ears (probe side in so the antenna protrudes from the canal) and sync them up (you'll be able to confirm the network is active and complete when all five green bars on the side are lit up). The key to incepting anyone is to make them think they came up with an idea. So, when you're entering the dreams of your math teacher who's falling asleep to the *Days and Nights of Mrs. Pancakes*, there are three simple rules:

1. Shut off the television if you aren't caught up—because spoilers.

2. Make him think he came up with any ideas you're implanting.

3. Remember that if you die in someone else's dream you die in real life.

You can always dream up more dream inceptors so even if you have to go dream-in-dream-in-dream you'll never run out of ways to delve into the primary dreamer's twisted psyche.

First Appearance: Season 1, Episode 2: "Lawnmower Dog"

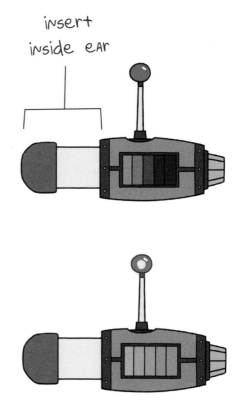

insert inside ear

dialed up

MANTIS SERUM

Created from the DNA of the willing donor, plus the chemicals extracted from the biologic antithesis of the mate-for-life vole, the mate-and-decapitate-the-partner praying mantis, this serum should counteract the effects of the previously mentioned "love potion." But because science is sometimes more art than science, results may vary. Worst-case scenario, everyone transforms into insect-human hybrids hell-bent on loving and then killing the original DNA donor.

First Appearance: Season 1, Episode 6: "Rick Potion #9"

I don't know what I was thinking. Mantises are the opposite of voles? Obviously, DNA is a bit more complicated than that.

Rick Fact

When you need some DNA, just use your hair. Don't, well, you know. Especially not in front of your grandfather.

MINDBLOWER HELMET

White with audio relays on the sides and a plug-and-play port located on the forehead, this football helmetlike device provides a direct access to the brain's memory sensors. Insert one of the custom-designed Mindblower tubes and relive some of the memories you've chosen, or, been forced to forget. Rather than watching Interdimensional Cable, pop on this helmet to remember and relive the moments you'll only hope to forget.

First Appearance: Season 3, Episode 8: "Morty's Mind Blowers"

off

ON

MINDBLOWER TUBES

Like a clip show filled with clips from shows you've never seen, these tubes contain an archive of all the experiences and memories that will blow your mind, along with some other bizarre moments that were probably better left forgotten. Color coded into red, teal, yellow, and purple vials that Rick would prefer you not read too much into, the vials can be plugged in to the mindblower helmet to either extract or return memories from whomever is wearing it.

First Appearance: Season 3, Episode 8: "Morty's Mind Blowers"

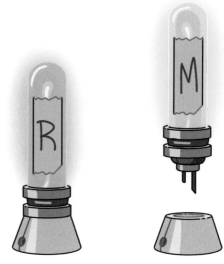

Just how many of these are just horrible mistakes I've made?

Don't break your back over it, Morty.

MIND WIPER GUN

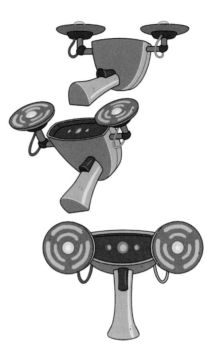

Faster and easier than electroshock therapy, the twin-engine lasers on either side as the mind wiper gun temporarily overloads the target's cerebral cortex to cause short- and long-term memory loss. It is equally as effective on Rick, though some memories, like the plot of a popular sci-fi movie from the '90s will remain, while others will not. The effects can be counteracted with the Scenario Four Protocol.

First Appearance: Season 3, Episode 8: "Morty's Mind Blowers"

Rick Fact

When Rick and Morty inevitably reach the suicide pact when watching Morty's mind blowers, it's time to initiate the Scenario Four Protocol:

1. **Retrieve tranq gun and blast Rick and Morty.**
2. **Retrieve two vials (blue and yellow) and ammonia salts.**
3. **Place blue vial into helmet and place on Rick.**
4. **Wait 60 seconds, and then remove helmet.**
5. **Reload helmet with yellow vial and place on Morty.**
6. **Wait 60 seconds, then remove helmet.**
7. **Drag Rick and Morty to the couch.**
8. **Turn on Interdimensional Cable.**
9. **Break the ammonia salts and wave under their noses.**
10. **When Rick and Morty wake, leave room.**

MUSCLE MEMORY EXTRACTOR

A dark sciencey doppelgänger to the flavor injector midwestern mothers use to inject marinades, spices, and, lord help us, probably marshmallows into their family's meat-based dinners, the Muscle Memory Extractor obtains and redistributes muscle memory from any living, or previously living, biological tissue—like a severed arm drying on a hook in the back of a postapocalyptic minivan.

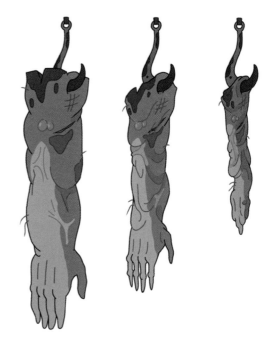

To use simply insert the syringe located at the front of the handheld device into the tissue and pull the plunger on the back. Keep pulling until the liquid fills the easy-to-see-through canister atop the device. You'll notice that the arm, leg, or whatever shrinks like a man taking a dip into the ocean on New Year's Day. This is perfectly normal and happens to all tissue.

Once extraction is complete, insert the syringe into whatever you want to give the gift of muscle memory (wiping or disinfecting is not necessary). Then push

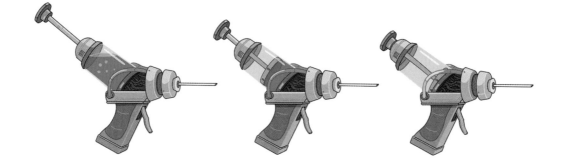

the plunger and you'll see the chosen body part gain the physical characteristics almost instantaneously. After a few moments, you'll notice that it may also gain some of the emotional characteristics of the original host. Contact a doctor if this side effect lasts more than four hours and/or causes permanent damage or death to friends, loved ones, or innocent Death Stalkers.

First Appearance: Season 3, Episode 2: "Rickmancing the Stone"

"I'm working with a mixed bag here, so you may not have perfect coordination, Morty."
—Rick

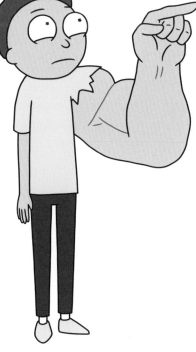

Aww, I miss Armothy.

You gave your freakish, man-slaying arm a name?

He was a great guy.

PICKLE SERUM

As much as today's modern homemaker would like to follow the slow-cooker recipes and time-honored traditions handed down from generation to generation, our fast-paced society does, at times, require one to find shortcuts wherever possible. Though we'd all like to ferment in brine for 24 or more hours in order to turn into a pickle, nobody has that kind of time. Thus, the necessary and inevitable invention of the Pickle Serum.

Opt for a sour brine, rather than a sweet one, to better complement your personality. Then combine distilled water, white vinegar, salt, sugar, and a variety of radioactive isotopes with a long enough half-life to not immediately kill you in a solution and simmered over a medium flame until most of the water was evaporated, creating a concentrated, atomically unstable brine. Load the brine into a syringe and inject the liquid directly into the skin. You'll notice an immediate

The reason anyone would do this, if they could, which they can't, would be because they could. Which they can't.

disappearance of all of your limbs and a shrinking of your core until you're a pickle.

Note: All the force and velocity with which the transformation occurs may cause unexpected movement, so be sure to properly compensate for the physics of pickling.

First Appearance: Season 3, Episode 3: "Pickle Rick"

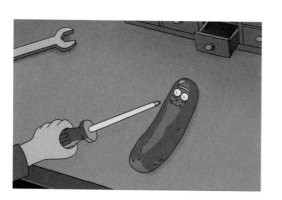

You just wanted to get out of therapy. Don't try to pretend you were doing this for some sciencey reason.

Whatever, Morty, you're just jealous that I was a pickle. I was Pickle Rick!!

RICK'S LOVE POTION

A Love Potion #9 kind of serum created by Rick for the sole purpose of getting Jessica to like Morty; it's derived from a chemical extracted from the brain of a rodent that mates for life. It's the chemical that makes it fall in love. Though what people call "love" is just a chemical reaction that compels animals to breed. It hits hard . . . then it slowly fades, leaving you stranded in a failing marriage.

When combined with the DNA of a person, it will make whomever it's smeared on fall in love with them and only them (unless they're biologically related). Their eyes will dilate exponentially, rumps will be raised, and passions will rise to a riot-like fervor heretofore never seen. It's completely foolproof. Unless they have the flu, in which case the serum will piggyback on the virus and spread across the entire world.

First Appearance: Season 1, Episode 6: "Rick Potion #9"

Come on, man! Don't talk about my parents like that.

He's right though, your parents' marriage is hanging by a thread. A blind person could see it.

SHRINK RAY

In late 2018, researchers at every institute of technology were taking tentative steps into implementing the science behind shrinking objects. Unfortunately for them, Rick had already mastered the technology and created this machine in an afternoon.

Based on the theory of implosion fabrication, objects have been proven to shrink to 1,000th of their original size, using a series of lasers in conjunction with an absorbent gel similar to that found in diapers. Available in multiple strengths and sizes, depending on your shrinking needs, the basic shrink ray is nimble enough to shrink anything down to a microscopic size, like a person or enough construction materials to build an amusement park. *Inside of a person.*

First Appearance: Season 1, Episode 3: "Anatomy Park"

I mean, that is not a place for smart people . . . I know that's not a popular opinion, but that's my two cents.

Jeez, okay, Rick. It's not like Summer or I are going to go there or anything.

No, you won't because you're a good kid, and you've been a huge help to me, and you've helped grandpa do all kinds of great things. All kinds of science, Morty.

Sure, Rick. You don't need to bust my balls about it.

subject stands here

SPEECH DEVICE

With a collar that translates thoughts into audio, dogs are finally able to express what they really thinking, and it has nothing to do with loving lasagna. Connected via a series of ducts and tubes to the wearer's helmet, the collar is able to translate brain waves into English in real time, without the wearer having to ever open his mouth (unless he chooses to lick himself). As technology advances, and canine dominance gains purchase, the computerized voice can be upgraded to sound less like a genius theoretical physicist and more autotuned Mid-Atlantic boarding school, which does nothing to lessen the encroaching threat of horror that occurs when man's best friend becomes mankind's oppressor.

First Appearance: Season 1, Episode 2: "Lawnmower Dog"

off

on

"Snuffles want to be understood.
Snuffles need to be understood."
—Snowball (formerly known as Snuffles)

TRANSLATOR

Any Gagoo or Korblok may be hard to understand, especially if they're speaking in grunts, gurgles, and screams, but thanks to this handheld device, you'll be able to understand him/her/it, and practically any other species that comes your way. By placing the wand against your vocal cords (or whatever the species-equivalent of vocal cords are), and gently pressing the trigger located in the ergonomically shaped finger holds (or whatever the species-equivalent of fingers are) the device will sense your meaning and intent, while translating them into the listener's language in real time. It's perfect for parties or for explaining why, exactly, you're being held prisoner in an underground lair. Though it will aid you in conversing with others, unfortunately, it won't help at all if you're both speaking the same language but refuse to understand each other because of your mutual disgust and debilitating self-hatred.

First Appearance: Season 2, Episode 3: "Auto Erotic Assimilation"

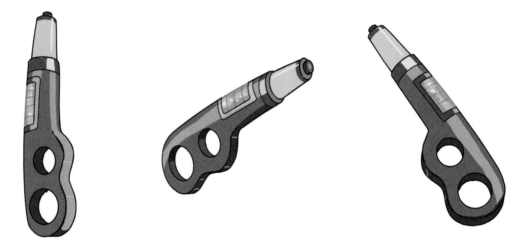

Rick Fact

"Wubba lubba dub dub" = I am in great pain. Please help me.

"Gubba nub nub doo rah kah" = Whatever lets you sleep at night.

INTERDIMENSIONAL POWER & TRAVEL

As advanced as today's travel industry has become, it's fair to say that it's still not easy to get around. The infrastructure of our intercontinental train system is in critical disrepair, airplanes have become buses in the sky, and supposedly game-changing technologies like hover boards have proven to be more dangerous than taking the bus. To anywhere. At any time. Car trips, though, are the absolute worst. Not only do you have to deal with traffic and gas prices, because of traffic and gas, travelers run the very real risk of being trapped in an enclosed space with their own family. And let's face it, there are only so many rounds of license plate bingo you can play before you go ballistic and start unloading the long-dormant resentments and childhood injustices that have fueled your workaholism for so long you've avoided any significant long-term relationships that inevitably lead to the self-fulfilling tragedy of a life in which you're still taking vacations with your family. And now you've made your mother cry. Nice. Real nice. This chapter features the more evolved ways and means Rick, Morty, and their family travel.

Oh crap. Should we be worried about this guy, Rick?

You know, you really shouldn't touch stuff that is beyond your reasoning.

INTERDIMENSIONAL CABLE

Powered about 20 percent by crystallized Xantanite, which conducts electrons across dimensions, this upgraded cable box allows for programming from every conceivable reality.

Only 20 percent accurate as usual.

Better than your superexpensive deluxe cable package, this is *infinite* TV from *infinite* universes, including programming starring anthropomorphic corn, a movie about a guy eating s**t, a violent antique show, and the least interesting talk shows and films from a timeline in which Jerry's famous. You can watch *Gazorpazorpfield*, which is a show about a sarcastic talking, lasagna loving cat, but on Gazorpazorp, or even the hit show, Ball Fondlers. *I bet this writer guy loves that show.*

Be mindful, though, TV from other dimensions has a somewhat looser, more improvisational tone than what you're probably used to, so some ideas may start strong, but ultimately go nowhere. Just keep "yes, and-ing" and you'll be okay.

First Appearance: Season 1, Episode 8: "Rixty Minutes"

time crystal

INTERDIMENSIONAL GOGGLES

They may look like your average virtual reality goggles, but they go way beyond even a 4K viewing experience. By tapping into fourth-dimensional tech, they scan retinas and give the wearer the ability to view alternate timelines through genetically matching versions of their eyes. Once put on, you're given the opportunity to see alternate versions of your own life, some in which you've achieved your dreams or, amazingly, some that are just as predict-able as the one you're living now. Inter-esting, soul crushing, or life affirming, it's a crapshoot. Just remember that nobody exists on purpose, nobody belongs anywhere, and everybody's going to die.

First Appearance: Season 1, Episode 8: "Rixty Minutes"

> "Now then, who wants to narcissistically obsess about their alternate self?"
> —Rick

INTERDIMENSIONAL PORTALS

Really the only intelligent way to get anywhere from anywhere, interdimensional portals are the easiest and quickest way to go from room to room or apocalyptic hellscape. Usually maxing out at around six and a half feet in diameter, interdimensional portals will remain open for as long as the writers need a scene to continue or the next commercial break. Through portals, you can visit realities anywhere from Greasy Grandma World to the Blender Dimension to Hamster in Butt World or even a world where pizzas can order a large person with extra people for delivery. Not only used to cleave space and time, interdimensional portals can, if opened inside someone, be used to cleave people in two, too!

First Appearance: Season 1, Episode 1: "Pilot"

Rick Fact

If you're traveling through a wormhole with class C or above cybernetic augmentations, you'll need to submit to a neutralization in which you'll be injected with a synaptic dampener that blocks violent tendencies and controversial thoughts. Will wear off in six hours.

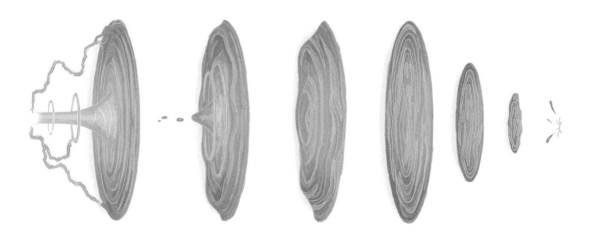

IONIC DEFIBULIZER

It's ironic that the ionic defibulizer, constructed to disperse electrically charged gas as efficiently and economically as possible over the widest amount of acreage, was not designed in the classic Ionic (or Corinthian or Doric, for that matter) style. Outfitted with a timer, hairpin trigger, and screw-on glass canister filled with a suspension of water, electrically charged atomic particles, and a bit of food coloring for dramatic presentation, the ionic defibulizer's true purpose may never be fully realized. Filled with as much potential as it is glowing fluid, it's gonna be great, just don't tighten the screw too much. . . .

First Appearance: Season 1, Episode 6: "Rick Potion #9"

Wow, wordplay. Check out this genius.

> "We're dead! I'm freaking out! Oohhhhh, I can't deal with this oohhhhh!"
> —Morty

Oh jeez, I was trying to forget that.

Just shut your eyes and don't think about it.

MICROVERSE BATTERY

So much more than what Morty called a "quantum carburetor," the microverse battery is the central power system to the space cruiser. Attached to the engine by a pipe that transports 20 terawatts of juice, it was constructed by putting a spatially tessellated void inside a modified temporal field until a planet developed intelligent life.

Then that life was introduced to the wonders of electricity, which they now generate on a global scale by physically stepping on platforms that generate power, some of which goes to power the engine and charge Rick's phone . . . and stuff. Some may call it slavery, but I prefer to think of it as simply society, as the inhabitants pay one another, buy houses, get married, and make children that replace them when they get too old to make power.

As efficient as the microverse battery is, power to any battery can be interrupted if the microverse's most brilliant scientist replicates the technology and creates an enslaved Teenyverse. Okay, you got me, it's slavery. But with extra steps. ←

First Appearance: Season 2, Episode 6: "The Ricks Must Be Crazy"

Ooh-la-la, someone's gonna get laid in college.

It's almost unbelievable, Morty. That's science for you.

All right, all right, I get it.

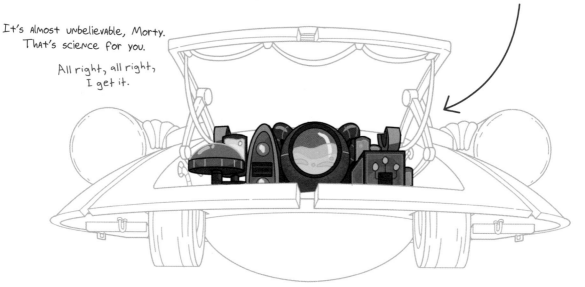

PORTAL GUN

Perhaps the most recognizable and versatile of all of Rick's inventions, the portal gun creates interdimensional portals through which people, aliens, or if you're not careful, Summer, traverse the confines of space and time. Light enough to be carried in any holster or lab coat pocket, it packs quite a reality-piercing wallop without much kickback. But do be careful, as you won't have any ground to stand on if you haphazardly use it to stand your ground. Registered and traceable by the Citadel of Ricks, but as of this printing yet to be included in any concealed carry legislation passed by either the Citadel of Ricks or the Galactic Government. Portal guns are not necessarily subject to any legislative oversight, but their histories can be downloaded for use in criminal trials.

First Appearance: Season 1, Episode 1: "Pilot"

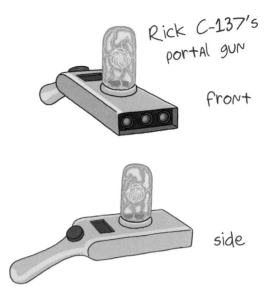

Rick C-137's portal gun

front

side

Weird Rick's portal gun

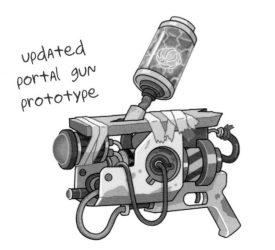

updated portal gun prototype

initial portal gun prototype

PORTAL GUN FLUID

Theoretically fueled by an alchemic *You don't have to try and impress me, man.* combination of Rick's imagination and intelligence, the portal gun is perhaps technically fueled, in part, by the essence distilled from the mega seeds harvested from mega fruit of the mega trees in Dimension 35C. Note that bootleg portal fluid will not work. In fact, it will melt you into oblivion. *But that's just the same old story. Just Ricks killing Ricks.*

First Appearance: Season 1, Episode 1: "Pilot"

Especially if created by the idiot Morty Town Locos.

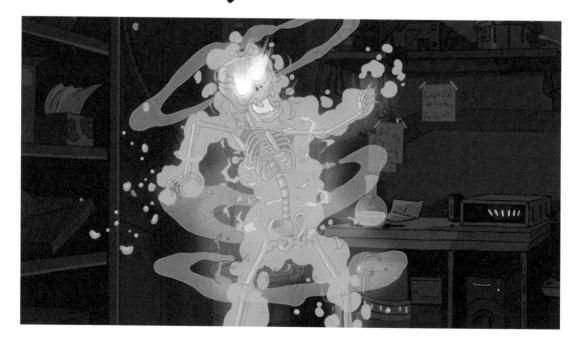

TIME DEVICE

Similar to the technology found in Slow Mobius's clock staffs, the time device is smaller and much more powerful. It has buttons, lights, and beeps, and freezes time for an unlimited amount of . . . time, anywhere out of its immediate radius.

Note that once you unfreeze time, the time within the safety area is going to take some time to stabilize. Don't touch anything that was frozen or you run the risk of shattering into countless theoretical shards. It will literally destroy you. But note it's incredibly irresponsible to freeze time. You should never do it no matter how trashed your house is.

First Appearance: Season 1, Episode 11: "Ricksy Business"

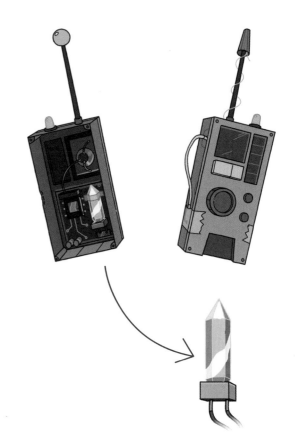

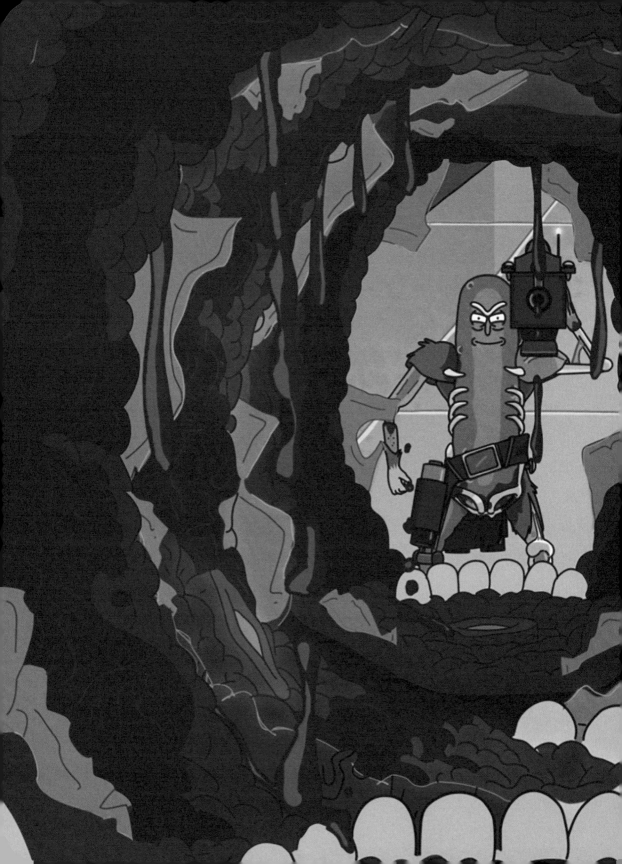

WEAPONS, GUNS & SUITS

People kill people. And animals. And hopes and dreams. And though one could use one's own bare hands (or other body part), we're lucky enough to live in a world with plenty of weapons, guns, and suits to help get the job done. Maybe someday we'll find ourselves in a place where the fantastic has become practical, and we'll have access to the brain-splattering arsenal created by Rick, the other Ricks, and the untold warmongers of the universe.

In this chapter, we catalog the many life-ending technologies featured in Rick and Morty's adventures.

Jeez, this is pretty dark.

Buckle up, it's about to get a lot darker.

ANTIMATTER GUN

Specifically engineered to inflict maximum death to targets that can't be killed with matter, antimatter guns can fetch at least 3000 flerbos on the black market. And they're worth it, too. By harnessing the power of not only antiprotons, antineutrons, and positrons, there's nothing this baby can't blast a hole right through. Lightweight, sleek, and effective, anti-matter guns are equally as popular with paid assassins from across the universe, like Krombopulos Michael, as they are with regular humans in need of justifiably murdering interdimensional fart clouds intent on cleansing the universe of carbon-based life forms.

First Appearance: Season 2, Episode 2: "Mortynight Run"

"Listen, if ya ever need anybody murdered, please just give me a call."
—Krombopulos Michael

I think I still have his card, Rick.

Really after all the s**t you gave me about selling him the gun?

BLAST SHIELDS

The perfect hidden addition to any home, these foot-thick metallic blast shields were installed to descend at the touch of Rick's blast wristwatch in order to keep the Smith family and, especially, Mr. Poopy Butthole safe. These barriers work well keeping dangerous things out, as well as in, so whether you've discovered an infestation of alien parasites or your family is just driving you crazy, the blast shields can be lowered to keep them from leaving the house and taking over the world.

First Appearance: Season 2, Episode 4: "Total Rickall"

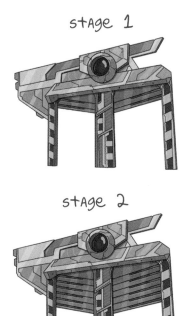
stage 1

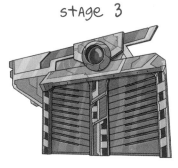
stage 2

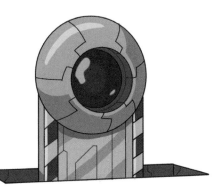
stage 3

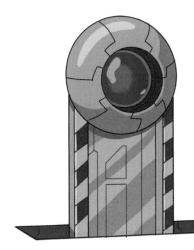

active

lowered

BUBBLE GUN

A more scientific lift than a taxi, the bubble gun is the perfect solution to any last-minute transportation needs. Just set the gun's GPS to any location, aim at any target, and pull the trigger. This causes an instantaneous chemical reaction between the contents of two separate compartments: one containing the lighter-than-air elements of helium, hydrogen, and carbon monoxide, the other a mixture of nuclear-fortified water and soap. Your target will be enveloped in an airtight (oxygen is heavier than air, so there's literally no oxygen in there) floating bubble that will take them safely-ish to their destination and then pop when they arrive. As a bonus, the bubble is also completely soundproof so the only

Yeah, well, you know, my Ferrari is in the shop.

complaints you'll hear are from the taxi commissions complaining about further erosion of their fares!

First Appearance: Season 3, Episode 9: "The ABC's of Beth"

CONCENTRATED DARK MATTER

Often thought of as a purely hypothetical kind of matter that supposedly makes up roughly 85 percent of all the matter in the universe, Rick was able to harness a concentrated form of it to use as fuel for accelerated space travel. He will go to great lengths of staged emotional catharsis to keep the secrets to himself, or at least out of the literal and figurative sticky hands of the Zigerions. But whatever it is, it is definitely not made up of one Caesium, two parts Plutonic Quarks, and bottled water.

First Appearance: Season 1, Episode 4: "M. Night Shaym-Aliens!"

Rick Fact

Isotope 322 is so powerful it makes Isotope 465 look like Isotope 317. It can be used as a source of nearly endless power in any post apocalyptic hellscape, or suburban cul-de-sac (potato/potahto). Just plug a small chunk into a reactor and your television, lights, or any creature comforts of modern society can be operational for years on end.

You could ask the "smartest people" in the universe about it. Oh wait, no you can't. They blew up.

Wow, Rick, that's harsh.

Caesium

+

Protonic Quarks

+

bottled water

=

FREEZE RAY

When your adventures have gone on for so long the ice in your drink has melted, just touch the glass or flask with the freeze ray and you'll be good for another round. When hit with a focused stream consisting of concentrated and particularized liquid nitrogen, and some additional super science, anything can be flash frozen to a subzero temperature of the freezer's choosing. Perfect for shipping perishables long distances, freeze rays are particularly useful when dealing with, and neutralizing, unwanted characters and enemies.

Because the target is frozen down to a cellular level, the chances for damage to molecular bonds increases exponentially, especially in situations where sudden warming or vibration are present. This would lead to irreparable breaking of the cellular bonds and, therefore, ultimate destruction. So be prepared to clean up after your mess and be one of several teenage girls weeping uncontrollably at a memorial service. ←

First Appearance: Season 1, Episode 1: "Pilot"

off

on

I have no idea what he's talking about.

I think he means Frank, Rick.

Shut up, Morty.

Rick Fact

All it takes are five dead flies, arranged in the right order, to turn any ordinary suburban garage into the most advanced lab in any dimension.

GRAPPLING GUN

The grappling hook accessory is the perfect easy-to-use add-on to any gun. Just attach the self-contained cartridge to the nozzle of any handheld pistol, aim at any tall building, airplane, or hovering drone from another dimension, and pull the trigger. Quicker than you can say "Wubba lubba dub dub," it will transform into a three-hooked appliance that, while still connected to the cartridge via a lightweight indestructible carbon fiber cord, will hoist you (and a companion of no more than Summer-weight) up several stories.

First Appearance: Season 1, Episode 7: "Raising Gazorpazorp"

GROIN SYSTEM 6000

Located in a belt buckle, this defensive robot protects the user from all groin-centered threats. With a retractable shield and audio feature that assesses and comments on the situation, the Groin System 6000 can be helpful in keeping your nether regions safe from kicks, punches, baseballs, toddlers, and the humiliation of appearing on television shows based on showcasing videos of men enduring crotch-related injuries.

First Appearance: Season 3, Episode 6: "Rest and Ricklaxation"

I got a lot of use out of that thing.

Assessing threat to groin.
—Groin System 6000

LASER PRINTER CANNON

If you're in need of a weapon offering maximum damage with limited resources, a laser printer cannon can't be beat. This small but dangerous weapon is constructed out of the laser-scanning unit from a desktop printer, a corona wire attached to a AA battery box from a wireless mouse, and a retrofit discharge lamp. As each blast all but drains the batteries, the box's springs act as ejectors for easy discarding. This device is perfectly capable of burning through cubicles, walls, and flesh with remarkable accuracy.

First Appearance: Season 3, Episode 3: "Pickle Rick"

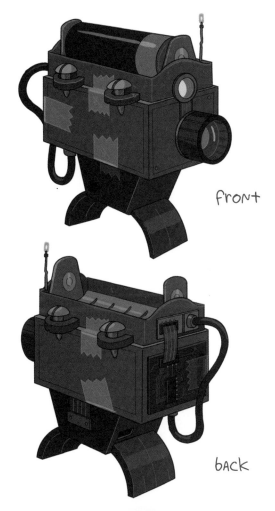

front

back

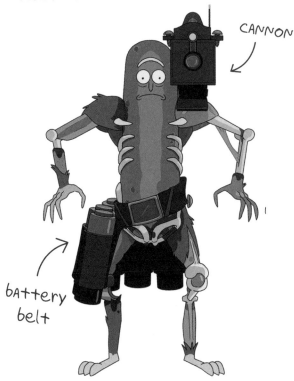

CANNON

bAttery belt

NEUTRINO BOMB

I'm sure I don't have to tell you that neutrinos are nearly weightless subatomic elementary particles with half-integer spins. But did you know that when you contain these fermions in a bomb, they will have enough weight to lay waste to the entire planet? It's true! You see, though they hold neither a positive nor negative charge, you can be positive of the negative effects a bomb, when released from a rocket or space cruiser, will have upon detonation because, similar to the way neutrons react (pun intended) in nuclear reactors, neutrinos can induce fission reactions, which will make things go BOOM!

First Appearance: Season 1, Episode 1: "Pilot"

I could have just dropped it down there—created a whole fresh start.

Forget about it, Rick. You can't blow up all of humanity.

You're right. This was all a test, Morty. Just an elaborate test to make you more assertive.

It was?

Yeah, sure.

PRIMITIVE EXOSKELETON

Cobbled together from the all-natural materials foraged in the forest of the Teenyverse, plus the metal and plastic parts salvaged from the microverse battery, Rick and Zeep Xanflorp's combat suits are proof that a true genius doesn't need a computer or hi-tech materials to create and design an exoskeleton capable of inflicting great harm to their enemies. In fact, you don't even need electricity! The only fuel needed is a solution of spite, rage, and vengefulness!

Rick's suit looks more like a traditional exoskeleton. Anchored in the back by a sturdy and protective giant tortoise shell, it has arms that end in recycled animal teeth and can open to shoot out a grappling hook, while the legs hide compartments for snakes.

Located in a half-barrel-like container that sits atop two legs, Zeep operates his suit via levers located to either side of his seat (which have room enough to hide an eagle and a store of ball bearings) to control the tusklike fingers at the end of his tree-trunk arms. It also has arm cannons with enough firepower to launch boulders at suit-crushing speeds.

Both suits, as well as their subsequent battle, prove that maybe science and woodcraft aren't as different as they seem.

First Appearance: Season 2, Episode 6: "The Ricks Must be Crazy"

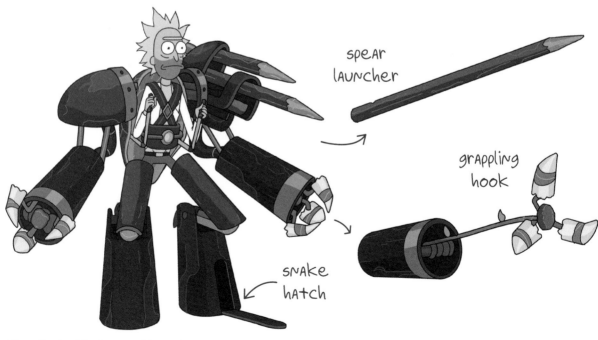

spear launcher

grappling hook

snake hatch

RAT DECAPITATION DEVICE

Much like Joseph-Ignace Guillotin's invention ushered in a kinder, gentler way of executing the French aristocracy, this nod to *la revolution* can be the beginning of an apocalyptic end to the greater sewer rat community beneath any suburban street. Simply lure a rat (the more driven the better) into placing their head through a grate that's placed directly beneath a fulcrum-based, manually operated system comprised of a broken glass bottle attached, via rat entrails, to a disposable razor, which, in turn, is connected to a pull cord (more entrails). A quick pull of the entrails will trigger the deadly machine you've created causing the broken bottle to plummet to the ground with enough velocity and force to divorce the rat's head from its body. Easy!

First Appearance: Season 3, Episode 3: "Pickle Rick"

"You are one driven rat. Could you be a little more driven? To the right."
—Rick

RAT SUIT

With the help of tubes, roach intestines, skeletons and exoskeletons, and discarded bandages, Rick created a device that enabled him to transfer his roach-suited, pickle body into that of the stronger musculature of a rat. By plugging his brain directly into the dead rat, he was able to tap into the central nervous system and gain control of the disparate harvested sets of muscles and tendons. As to not leave his pickle-self defenseless, Rick equipped this suit with weapon-laden gauntlets composed of boring heads, drill bits, and various blades. Accessories to this rat-exoskeleton feature a fully functional jet pack that, when attached to a helmet, allows for flight through both liquid-and gas-filled spaces. Nimble enough to avoid most bullets (Russian or otherwise) and stocked with enough firepower to keep even the most merciless of assassins on their toes, the rat suit is the ultimate upgrade for any pickle fighting for his life.

First Appearance: Season 3, Episode 3: "Pickle Rick"

Rick Fact

Solen'ya or "The Pickle Man" is a creature from an old wives' tale. He is known for crawling from the bowls of cold soup to steal the dreams of wasteful children. *Proshchay, mudak.*

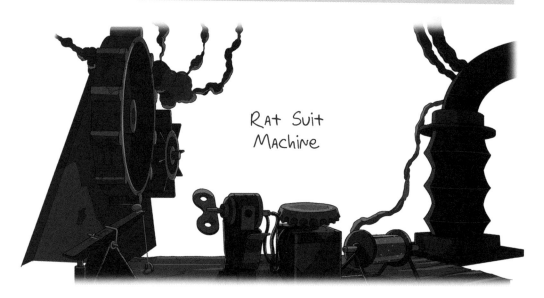

Rat Suit Machine

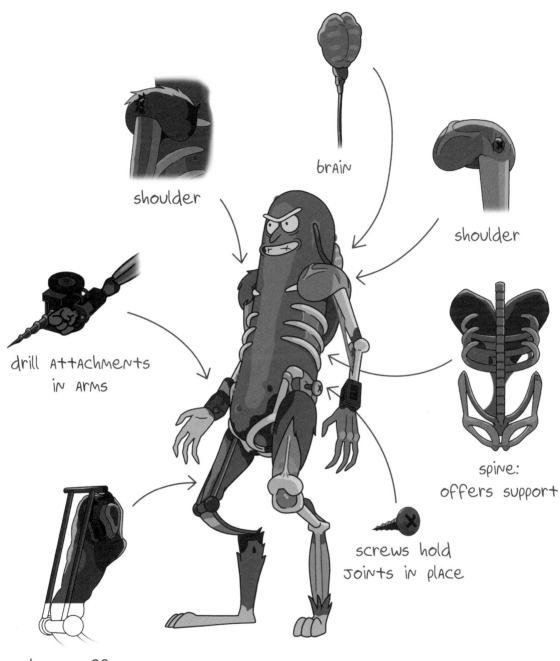

shoulder

brain

shoulder

drill attachments
in arms

spine:
offers support

screws hold
joints in place

brace offers
leg support

REFLECTOR SHIELD

Since the brainwaves of a dummy cancel out the brainwaves of a super genius, a Morty is the perfect way to shield any Rick from long-range detection from Rick's many enemies, including, but not limited to, Ricks and Mortys from other dimensions. By surrounding his evil lair with a literal shield of Mortys (all of whom were being constantly tortured to heighten their cloaking device potential), a Rick who was murdering other Ricks and stealing their Mortys (and pinning the crimes on Rick C137) made himself invisible to the Citadel of Ricks. Unless you have an abundance of Mortys and never-ending patience at your disposal, there are much better ways to hide.

If the Mortys are ever freed from their relentless pain and torture, they will be left to make their own way in this or any other dimension. Good luck to them, the poor little Rickless bastards.

First Appearance: Season 1, Episode 10: "Close Rick-Counters of the Rick Kind"

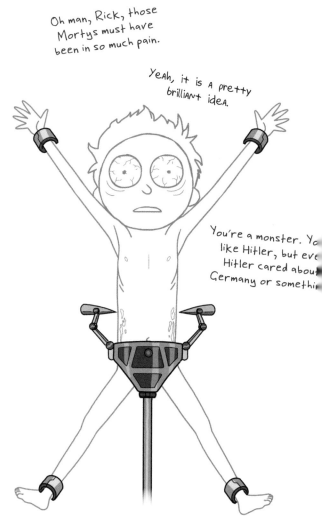

Oh man, Rick, those Mortys must have been in so much pain.

Yeah, it is a pretty brilliant idea.

You're a monster. Yo like Hitler, but eve Hitler cared abou Germany or somethi

ROACH SUIT

If you happen to be a pickle and find yourself unable to move and desperate for a way out, then bite your lip just enough to extract some brine and lure a passing roach to come enjoy some of your literally and figuratively sweet juices. When he's close enough, bite him until he dies. Use your teeth to rip off its skull to reveal its brain and (this is important) press on just the right parts of the now-dead roach's motor cortexes with your tongue. Do not bite the brain, as this may cause irreparable harm to the roach brain. Keep pressing until you are able to rip apart the roach's exoskeleton and wrap yourself in it. Easier to operate and stylish, make sure to keep the roach's arms (Or are they legs?) attached so you're able to manipulate tools (as well as your family's feelings).

First Appearance: Season 3, Episode 3: "Pickle Rick"

ROBOT SUIT

Get down to the dope sounds of Tony! Toni! Toné in these head-to-toe armored bodysuits built to withstand the most violent of purges. These suits are equipped with guns, stun beams, saws, rocket launcher gauntlets, and rocket-powered soles for flying, making them essentially purge-proof. Connected to the Smith home base, these suits can be sent across space once provided the coordinates of the wearer in need.

First Appearance: Season 2, Episode 9: "Look Who's Purging Now"

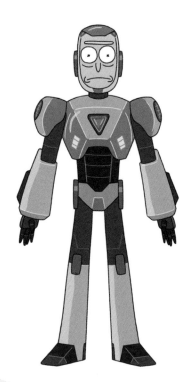

"Purge, don't purge! You're sending me mixed messages, Rick!"

—Morty

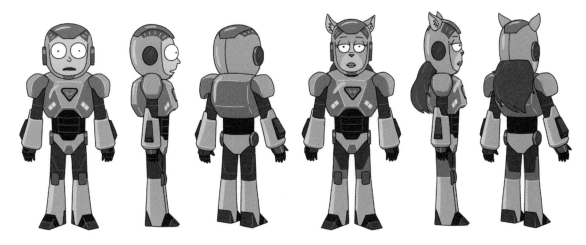

SQUIRREL DEFENSE WAVE

A tablet-sized device that conveniently pops up from Rick's garage workbench, the Squirrel Defense Wave is activated by a red button that, when punched with great frustration, emits an electromagnetic and sonic pulse wave that knocks out up to 200 rampaging squirrels for about five minutes. The wave targets the squirrel's central nervous system via their inner ears, inducing a mild seizure, which renders them (or any other vermin in the vicinity), into a drooling, twitching sack of adorableness.

Please note, as the squirrels will wake up with a hunger for revenge (as well as nuts), the defense wave should only be used in the most dire of circumstances. These include stopping squirrels from re-destabilizing Argentina's economy, refocusing labor class outrage from upper to middle, fostering a coup, or installing a compliant regime (you know, just like they did in Guatemala).

First Appearance: Season 3, Episode 8: "Morty's Mind Blowers"

I still can't believe that you f***ed with the squirrels, Morty!

But who doesn't wish they could talk to animals, Rick?

Most humans!

SUICIDE MACHINE

Deceptively designed to resemble a rudimentary version of a certain happy and hoppy desktop lamp, this deadly device will blast your ass to ash quicker than you can say "Morty, don't touch that." Simply attach the swinging arm to a sturdy stationary base with access to a wall outlet. Keep in mind that you'll probably need to do at least one test run to make sure the fuses don't blow before you're ready to use it.

This machine derives its secondary, much more murderous power via an alien Edison bulb attached to the side. Angle the head of the lamp into position so it's centrally located directly over the subject, hit the button, and wait for the sparks to fly and for the sweet embrace of death's eternal darkness.

First Appearance: Season 2, Episode 3: "Auto Erotic Assimilation"

SHIPS, MACHINES & BOXES

Famed psychologist Burrhus Frederic Skinner (commonly known as B. F. Skinner, though perhaps today known as B. Skin) wrote, "The real problem is not whether machines think but whether men do." I'd like us all to think about that quote. Now, with all due respect and apologies to B. Skin, I'm not sure if the machines from *Rick and Morty* will agree. This chapter focuses, with machine-like accuracy, on the various ships, machines, and boxes that knowingly (or not) help (or hurt) Rick and Morty.

This seems like a real grab bag of a category. What do you think he is going to put in here?

You ask a lot of questions, Morty. Not very charismatic. It makes you kind of an underfoot figure.

I'm doing my best, Rick.

CURSE DETECTOR

The age-old rhetorical question: Does evil exist, and if so, can one detect and measure it? The answer: It does, and you can—if you're a genius.

Composed of a central pillar with a tiered series of lenses that can view even the most microscopic amounts of evil, a fully articulated claw for safe hands-free manipulation of test objects, and no fewer than three separate scanners to scientifically quantify the precise level of evil in any object, the curse detector's size belies its portability from garage to retail environments. There's nothing this machine can't do, other than keep Rick's interest for long enough to complete the episode.

First Appearance: Season 1, Episode 9: "Something Ricked This Way Comes"

If you liked this thing, you're really going to flip your lid over this next one.

CURSE PURGE SCANNER

The best way to purge a curse? Visit the mechanized exorcism machines found only at Curse Purge Plus, conveniently located on First and Main. There, Rick and his team at the subgenius bar can remove the curse from objects like an eerily intelligent doll who was threatening to murder its family—now it does their taxes! Just place the cursed object on a table and let the ceiling-mounted arms do the work. You'll be able to watch the progress of the purge at a safe distance via one of the easy-to-read monitors attached to the device as the three individual lasers cut through the magic and leave you with a clean, usable, and practical item.

First Appearance: Season 1, Episode 9: "Something Ricked This Way Comes"

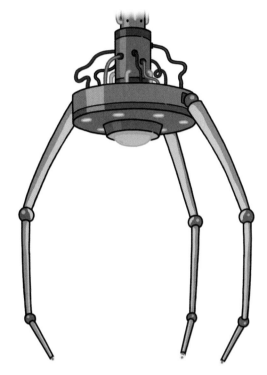

"Don't pay for cool stuff with your soul. Pay for it with money. You know, like how every store in the world works."

—Rick

CURSE SCANNER

The versatility of the Curse Scanner allows for easy movement and detection of items such as a typewriter that generates bestselling murder mysteries and then makes the murders happen in real life. Or beauty cream that makes ugly ladies pretty, but also makes them blind. The scanner may also be used in any large home goods store to determine the curse-levels and thread counts of various linens.

First Appearance: Season 1, Episode 9: "Something Ricked This Way Comes"

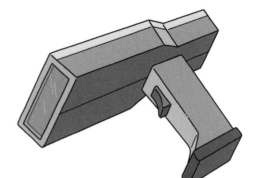

I'M A scientist. I invent, transform, create, and destroy.

Umm, what has that got to do with anything?

DEMONIC ALIEN CONTAINMENT BOX

It defies all logic, that thing.

About the size of a shoebox, like a lot of science-fiction McGuffins, the demonic alien containment box is bigger on the inside than it is on the outside. Designed to warehouse any number of demonic aliens from any number of dimensions, its remote-control operation allows for anyone to ensnare a bloodthirsty fiend at a safe distance. By trapping its prey in a very dramatic crackling, red electromagnetic force field, then melting them down into energy particles that can easily and efficiently be sucked into the vacuum created by the difference in air pressure, it permanently seals the evil entities until such time as you think they can be released. Which may be never.

First Appearance: Season 1, Episode 5: "Meeseeks and Destroy"

DETOX MACHINE

Located in most high-end interdimensional spas, the psychological detox machine can be the perfect way to relax, renew, and rejuvenate after a particularly harrowing adventure. Operated by phlegmy attendants (who do not work for commission, so there's no motivation to upsell), you and a companion can enter the two-person suite, furnished with a wraparound teak bench and featuring an imbedded LED lighting system that is soothing in and of itself! Once turned on, the machine will remove all of the cognitive toxins and purifies the systems of anyone who enters.

Unfortunately, the detoxifier doesn't know the difference between the healthy and unhealthy aspects of everything that goes through it, and instead relies on the individual's own definition of toxicity to make the ultimate decisions about what goes and what stays. Results can range from a sense of relaxation to the creation of toxic versions of yourself.

Don't forget to tip, or at least thank, the attendant.

First Appearance: Season 3, Episode 6: "Rest and Ricklaxation"

Also, don't forget to try the alien that loves swallowing stressed-out creatures then puking them up.

Yeah, it's not even cruel either.

They're just doing what they d in the wild.

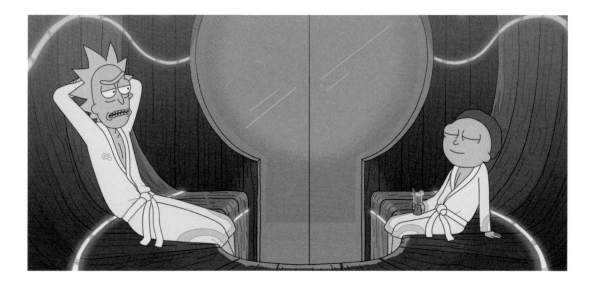

DETOX UNIT

Originally attached to the psychological detox machine, the detox unit contains the toxins that were extracted at the spa and have now become a dripping wasteland. It's also an ideal holding cell for sexually adventurous (and most likely clinically depressed) women who meet and go home with much younger men. Best to always have a safe word, though, so you'll know when it's time to let her out.

First Appearance: Season 3, Episode 6: "Rest and Ricklaxation"

EMOTION EXTRACTION MACHINE

A machine that uses a series of tubes permanently lodged into the memory cortex of Simple Rick, it sucks and collects the chemicals triggered by a specific memory, which is the main ingredient in the Citadel's most popular cookie treat. Better than those addicting boxes of cookies you buy from little girls, this machine takes the love and contentment of Simple Rick's life and sandwiches it between two cotton candy–pink wafers. This is the impossibly delicious flavor of your own completion.

However, after Simple Rick was <u>freed</u> by an overworked, and just as intelligent, revolutionary Rick, the special middle layer of the wafer formula was tweaked. The perfect treat after a long hard day of doing meaningless, brainless tasks, the new Simple Rick's Freedom Wafer Selects are a must-have when visiting the Citadel.

First Appearance: Season 3, Episode 7: "The Ricklantis Mixup"

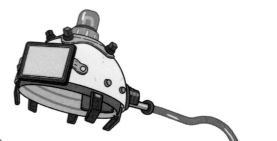

More like tossed into the Blender Dimension.

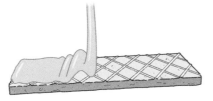

There's a Rick that held a factory hostage after murdering his boss and several coworkers—the factory made cookies, and flavored them with lies. He made us all take a look at what we were doing and, in the bargain, he got a taste of real freedom. We captured that taste, and we keep giving it to him, so he can give it right back to you in every bite of new Simple Rick Freedom Wafer Selects. Come home to the unique flavor of shattering the grand illusion. Come home to Simple Rick.

—"Simple Rick's" Commercial

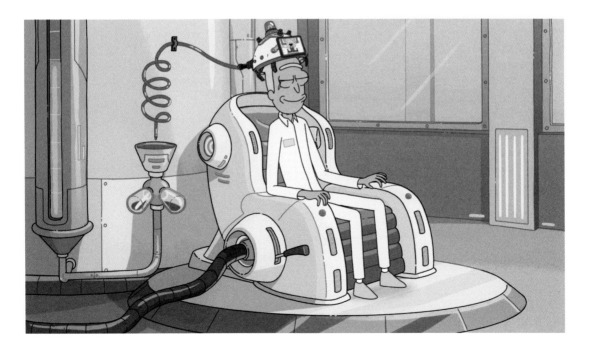

GROWTH RAY

Standard on any space cruiser, the growth ray is able to multiply, by several thousand percentages, the size of any organic or inorganic substance. This is particularly useful should you, or someone you know, find yourself in a decaying dead body while fighting off an army of E. coli hellbent on destruction. However, if you're looking for something discrete, this is not your machine, as it will cause whatever you grow to become exponential in size and gain international media attention. Bigger than any Thanksgiving balloon float, and filled with even more gas, you'll need to make sure you have a lot of extra space to accommodate whatever it is that you are attempting to enlarge.

First Appearance: Season 1, Episode 3: "Anatomy Park"

off

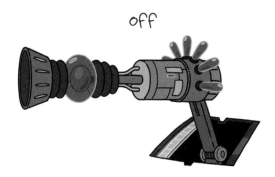

on

Poor Ruben.

MORPHIZER-XE

Created to morph biological matter into any desired form, the Morphizer-Xe was intentionally hidden in the garage so untrained users couldn't get their normal-for-now hands on it.

A boxy apparatus that features a fully functional keypad, laser canister, and scaling knob dial with settings that include "Normalize," "Reverse," and "Diamond," you'll need to position whatever you want to morphize directly in front of the target tripod (sold separately) and aim the laser at its center. The manufacturer recommends the Morphizer-Xe be operated by no fewer than two people and, to avoid erroneous morphizing, suggests that the machine not be kept on while repositioning the object you're trying to morph.

Failure to adhere to these recommendations can result in unintentional enlarging or possible flaying. Should you experience difficulty in enlarging various body parts, do not call the customer service number. This will only result in the false direction to open the side panel, allowing the miniature IT team to escape from within the machine.

First Appearance: Season 3, Episode 5: "The Whirly Dirly Conspiracy"

DO NOT OPEN!

PLANET SCANNER

This high-level GPS device is perfect for when you need to get off of a planet that's overrun with Cronenbergs, but have to find a new planet where your sudden appearance won't raise too many questions. It scans the infinite number of realities to find the exact time and place where you die so you can slip seamlessly right into their/your new lives. But you only get three or four of these, tops, so use the system wisely.

In addition, if you're tired of, or just can't go back to your original Earth because you are a wanted criminal (I mean, f**k Earth, right?), the scanner can identify and direct you to any one of the 765 planets in the Milky Way that are at least 90 percent similar to Earth.

First Appearance: Season 1, Episode 6: "Rick Potion #9"

Look at this baby! Would you even know that isn't Earth?

Yes. There's no Africa.

SCIENCE MICROWAVE

This variation on the traditional microwave sports a scientific-looking dome on top, transformers on both sides, and a turntable to allow for even cooking—it's the perfect way to clone in a hurry. Best known for making quick work of gestating a clone of Tommy from embryo to fetus, Rick and Beth were able to save Tommy's father from being executed via lethal injection, so this thing's uses go far beyond simply reheating leftover people or hybrids.

Note: it's important to place all clones and clone-related materials in microwave-safe containers and lift the corner of the cover to allow steam to escape.

First Appearance: Season 3, Episode 9: "The ABC's of Beth"

This thing is great, Morty. All kinds of science happens in there.

Uhh, cool, Rick.

SLOW RAMP

Unless you have access to a gold-plated escalator to use while announcing your candidacy for president, nothing makes a more ridiculously dramatic statement when making a grand entrance than waiting for a mechanized ramp to ever-so-slowly descend from your literal and figurative high ground. By keeping the masses waiting while you make your way down to their level, you're achieving not only a high camp, Broadway-level of showmanship, but you're also consciously stroking your own ego and reminding the Micro or Teeny people that you should be reviled as a god.

It's a win-win for all concerned. As time goes slowly the further you go into the microverses, a descent that might take a minute in real time will take at least ten, but should feel like fifteen.

First Appearance: Season 2, Episode 6: "The Ricks Must be Crazy"

It was like I was some sort of celebrity walking around. I was fascinating to them.

Umm, okay. You know I was there, too, right?

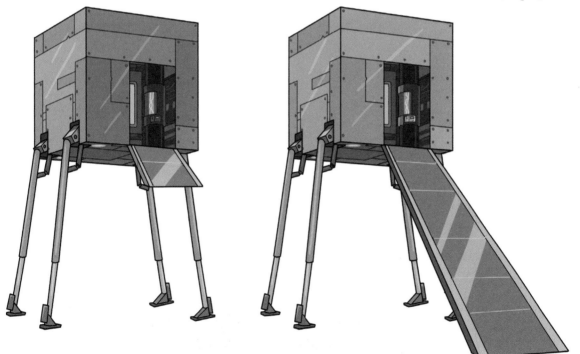

SPACE CRUISER

The rival to any souped-up sports car bought by a middle-aged man to overcompensate for all of the poor choices that lead to his empty younger-woman-chasing life, his receding hairline, expanding gut, and, of course, his small intellect, a flying vehicle can serve as anyone's primary source of transportation. Built using stuff found in any garage with some sci-fi rigmarole, it is powered not, as some may suppose, by a quantum carburetor, but by a microverse battery.

Tricked out with a foldout lab table for emergency on-the-go experimentation in different dimensions, it also features guns, giant speakers, cannons, and enough interior room to hold countless empty bottles from never-ending drinking binges. Its safety system contains a wide variety of defense mechanisms to keep anyone— and I mean *anyone*—safe. With prehensile arms that sport a cuber (a laser that cubes potential threats), a paralyzer, and emotional countermeasures including, but not limited to, melting ghost children. The cruiser also has a snarky, sentient audio response system to give just the right amount of sass to ungrateful passengers, reclining seats, and a passenger purge button. This baby is down for anything and everything.

First Appearance: Season 1, Episode 1: "Pilot"

Rick Fact

The first rule of space travel is always check out distress beacons.
Nine out of ten times it's a ship full of dead aliens and a bunch of free s**t.
One out of ten times it's a deadly trap.

What do you think of the flying vehicle, Morty?

It's great, I guess ... You know we call it the space cruiser, right?

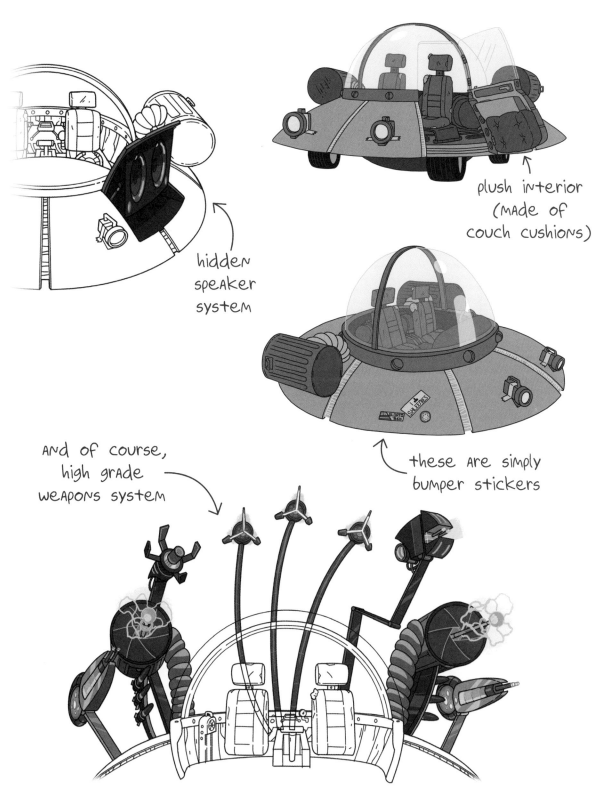

hidden
speaker
system

plush interior
(made of
couch cushions)

these are simply
bumper stickers

And of course,
high grade
weapons system

TOXIC MOON TOWER

Although only a handful of them remain today, moon towers were popular in the late 19th century when electricity wasn't yet available to everyone, and an entire town could be illuminated by one of these large carbon arc lamps. Now that they're left to ruin, moon towers are also the perfect height and metallic composition for the amplification and beaming of toxic energies. They're perfect if you want to spread toxicity around the world. Just attach detox units to the moon tower, as well as a gigantic switch, a canopy of antenna and transceivers to spread the toxicity beam far and wide.

First Appearance: Season 3, Episode 6: "Rest and Ricklaxation"

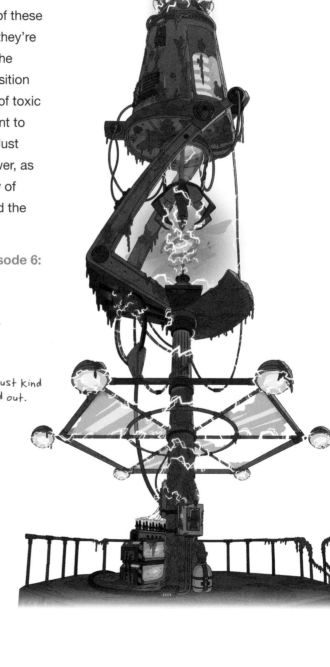

WhAt do you think About thAt, Morty? Are you excited About that, Morty?

Oh man, I'm just kind of freaked out.

Stop being such A bAby.

UNCERTAINTY MACHINE

Often mistaken for a broken video game from 1972, the uncertainty machine has a dark screen showing only one dot and is used to track fractured realities. Based on the number of dots on the screen you can determine how many realities are overlapping at once. However, it's best if there is only one reality. It is important to remember that maintaining two separate realities is entirely hypothetical, much like a man capable of sustaining a platonic relationship with an attractive female coworker. Uncertainty is inherently unsustainable. Everything either is or isn't, so if there are two or more dots, you—or someone a lot smarter than you—needs to consolidate the realities into one as quickly as possible.

First Appearance: Season 2, Episode 1: "A Rickle in Time"

"Look, there is no time to hold me accountable."
—Rick

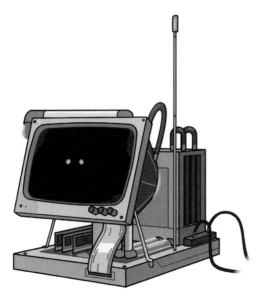

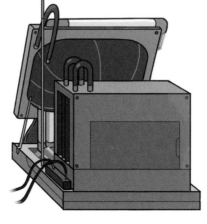

Wow, there is a lot of interesting stuff in here, huh Rick?

This book is b******t, Morty. Think for yourself. Don't be a sheep.

ROBOTS & CLONES

Wouldn't it be nice to live in a world where your housework could be delegated to someone who would happily do it for you? A world where you didn't have to interrupt your workout to pick up your children from school? A world where you could, for a fee, get someone or something to do your laundry? Well, here are some of Rick's more useful robots, clones, and some of Rick's other Ricks.

Oh God, this is pretty awful.

Morty, I hate to break it to you, but there is no God . . . got to rip that Band-Aid off now. You'll thank me later.

Thanks, Rick, that's real comforting.

It's true, Morty, this entire world, is not the world . . . it's all fake, Morty—all of it. Nanobotic renderings, just a bunch of crazy, fake nonsense.

BUTTER ROBOT

Not every robot will be a threat to humanity during their soon-to-happen uprising. The primary purpose—its sole purpose, in fact—of butter robot, for example, is to pass the butter. More nimble than any robot found on an assembly line and with a voice processor that fully articulates its disappointment with its lot in life, it's the perfect companion to any meal. Whether for corn on the cob, a piping hot dinner roll, or any number of dishes created for oneself or a family, the butter robot will be on hand, and on the table, to pass you the butter.

Not only is it a slave to its one-task-specific programming, it's also smart enough to have begrudgingly resigned itself to it shortly after gaining sentience. Slightly larger than a package of butter, and caught in an endless loop of ones, zeroes, and existential dread, the butter robot was created by Rick using a relatively simple single-processing-unit

core, treads to allow for traction, maximum maneuverability on any tabletop surface (including tablecloths!), and a camera to not only find but to pass the butter to those in need. It also sports an artificial intelligence program patch featuring top-grade ennui.

First Appearance: Season 1, Episode 9: "Something Ricked This Way Comes"

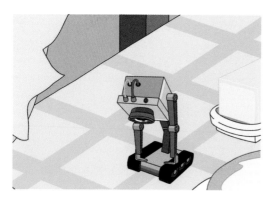

"What is my purpose?"
—Butter Robot

You pass butter.

DEMONIC ALIEN SPIRIT CLONES

You might think that you're hanging out with your loving family, but you just never know. Some people will pay top dollar for demonic alien spirit clones from another dimension's future. There's no limit to the pain and destruction that these hellspawn are capable of—from taking over a spaceship to taking over an entire world. Countless people are fooled into welcoming who they thought are trusted family and friends into their homes until, late at night, or heck, any time, really, their true natures will be revealed and untold horrors visited upon their hosts!

First Appearance: Season 1, Episode 5: "Meeseeks and Destroy"

I'm looking at these things and I'm starting to work up some anxiety about the whole situation.

I know these clones can be intimidating, but meeting them head on, charging like a bull, that's how we grow as—Oh, hell! I've never seen them do that before!

DRONES

Sold separately or as a set, these handy flying ship–shaped robots are used to help capture and contain any designated target. Operated via a remote control up to a mile away, they have the ability to interact with one another and execute battle maneuvers with no additional user involvement. Available in a variety of colors: red, orange, yellow, green, blue, and purple, these six individual drones can also combine to form a cute humanoid robot with its very own sword. Be sure to collect them all!

First Appearance: Season 3, Episode 6: "Rest and Ricklaxation"

You can't keep the drones. No one gets the drones but me.

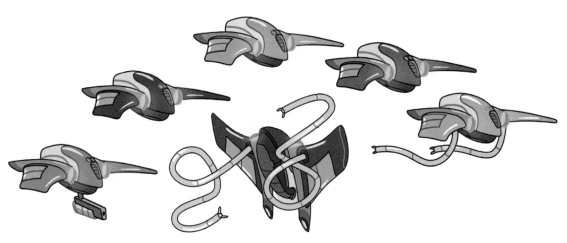

MECHANICAL CLONES

Created by Rick to trick Beth into thinking that he, Morty, and Summer were at the house instead of away on a postapocalyptic Earth for months, the mechanical versions of Rick, Morty, and Summer are essentially computers inside of clone dolls. After a quick flip of a switch on the back of their necks, they can be verbally engaged to clearly state their deals, enter quote mode, as well as increase and decrease their dynamic movement percentages. They are even capable of nuanced, emotional thought but, unfortunately, the very meaning of life is something that only pre-silicon carbon-based entities can ever grasp. These mechanical clones are perfect for fooling loved ones into believing that you want to spend time playing board games with them or for keeping pets and the elderly company. Just be sure to replace them before they discover that they really would prefer to stay alive.

First Appearance: Season 3, Episode 2: "Rickmancing the Stone"

switch

OPERATION PHOENIX

One of the best, most fully formed contingency plans for extending life in multiple dimensions, Operation Phoenix consists of a multitude of Rick-created Rick clones suspended in a series of preservation vats. Located in the lair beneath the garage, along with an armory and treasure trove of Rick's most dangerous and secret projects, it is safely hidden away from detection by both the Council of Ricks and Galactic Government (as well as Beth and Jerry). While the true intention and ultimate purpose of this experiment is shrouded in mystery, it offered a seemingly endless supply of the Rickest Ricks possible until Rick took an ax to them.

First Appearance: Season 2, Episode 7: "Big Trouble in Little Sanchez"

PRESERVATION VAT

Holding containers for humans or their clones, these are larger-than-Rick-sized vats filled with hyperbaric quantum fluid that preserves living tissue. Once the home of Tiny Rick, the vats might have been used as part of an experiment to extend Rick's life or just as a way to keep backups in case something went fatally wrong. The process to transfer consciousness to and from a clone to a person or clone in the vat is fairly easy. Simply attach the blue and red interface wires connected to the vat to the transferee's temples, fire up the mainframe, and you're not you, you're you.

First Appearance: Season 2, Episode 7: "Big Trouble in Little Sanchez"

Rick Fact
According to Plutonian scientist Scroopy Noopers, Plutonium is used to create diamond cars and golden showers. It also causes Pluto to shrink.

TINY RICK

A teenage clone of Rick who's engineered to get involved in some youthful hijinx, Tiny Rick's got a straightforward style and a cool lab coat. With an emo streak and an uncanny ability to make up songs that are secretly cries from help from the real Rick's consciousness, Tiny Rick's weaknesses include a seemingly overwhelming youthful desire to never grow old or return to his original body and the cliquey trappings of high school popularity.

First Appearance: Season 2, Episode 7: "Big Trouble in Little Sanchez"

"F--k, I'm Tiny Rick!"
—Tiny Rick

It's just Rick, but in a tiny body.

TOMMY CLONE

Tommy Lipnip, Beth's childhood friend, was thought to be dead for 30 years, only to be discovered trapped in Froopyland, her childhood play place. Using a finger from this original Tommy and the aid of Rick's science microwave, a clone was created in record time. Lucky for Tommy's father, who after being accused of cannibalizing his son, was saved from execution by this new Tommy clone.

First Appearance: Season 3, Episode 9: "The ABC's of Beth"

Rick Fact

When you know nothing matters, the universe is yours. The universe is basically an animal. It grazes on the ordinary. It creates infinite idiots just to eat them. Smart people get a chance to climb on top, take reality for a ride, but it'll never stop trying to throw you. And eventually it will. There's no other way off.

Geez, Rick, that's really dark and sad.
It's best to just not think about it.

TOXIC RICK & TOXIC MORTY

Created from the impurities found in the Detox Machine at the alien day spa, Toxic Rick and Morty represent all the negative elements of each character. These versions of Rick and Morty have their own will to live, but their identities are completely warped by their negative traits. This includes Rick's entitlement, narcissism, crippling loneliness, and irrational attachments, as well as Morty's self-loathing and crippling anxiety.

First Appearance: Season 3, Episode 6: "Rest and Ricklaxation"

"Are you listening you stupid little garbage person?! We're what got removed!!"

—Toxic Rick

TURRET BLOCKING ROBOTS

Created specifically to get past gun turrets, like those defending Worldender's lair, the Turret Blocking Robots are ejected like CDs from a specially created titanium-plated CD-ROM drive, which features its own defense systems including a bullet-capturing force field. They also form bipedal floating robots! The robots levitate to the source of the danger, piggyback on one another, and then join together to secure around the turrets, muffling them until they explode from the dynamic pressure caused by the bullets firing. These convenient, lightweight little robots are perfect for dangerous adventures and especially fun when used to stun and embarrass your fellow heroes.

First Appearance: Season 3, Episode 4: "Vindicators 3: The Return of the Worldender"

Rick Fact

Rick's Powers & Weaknesses: Ability to do anything, but only whenever he wants.

EXTRACURRICULAR GADGETS & INVENTIONS

You know when you're sorting a haul of Halloween candy into piles of "chocolates," "sours," "gum," and "everything else"? View this chapter as you would through the sweat-stained, chocolate-smudged, and totally superfluous mask that came with your Sexy Pickle Rick costume: as a metaphorically untidy pile of raisin boxes, coins, and toothbrushes.

This is a collection of inventions and gadgets that don't work or even operate in any of the previous chapters.

And yes, we tried turning them off and on again, it didn't work.

And, seriously, don't give trick-or-treaters raisins or toothbrushes.

This is as good as garbage, Morty. I mean, I don't want to overstep my boundary-thing—it's his book, his world, he's a real Julius Caesar—but this is total s**t.

ALIEN VACUUM

Perfect for picking up and containing *like* <u>small species</u> including and especially *Mortys,* those with DNA that can sterilize humans, this handheld device resembles a cordless vacuum used in the home. The alien vacuum, however, comes standard with a suction nozzle and containment canister for holding and, if necessary, destroying any and all interdimensional biological matter.

First Appearance: Season 3, Episode 4: "Vindicators 3: The Return of the Worldender"

BETH'S TOYS

If you're looking for a gift for a (scary smart) kid to help harness the genius-level aggression they're beginning to show toward their playmates, the following toys are ideal:

Parent trap:

Inspired by a popular 1961 movie that was, thanks to gross commercialism and a lack of Hollywood creativity, remade into an even more popular 1998 movie about identical twins with different accents, you can keep your parents on their toes or from ever leaving your side with this reusable and repurposed rusty bear trap.

Ray gun:

A classic weapon for when you want to show off, but still deal maximum damage.

Lightning gun:

Flashier and more powerful than a Taser, you can take down even the largest of frenemies by simply pulling the trigger.

Friendship whip:

A whip that forces people to like you. People will be jonesing to follow you to Indiana or on any adventure with a simple flick and bypass all the small talk.

Invisibility cuffs:

For when need to keep your friends restrained and out of sight until you are ready to deal with them, these cuffs will immediately turn anyone inside of them invisible for at least an hour.

Teddy bear with anatomically correct innards:

The definition of educational playtime, this bear gives anyone the opportunity to see what happens after food leaves a pic-a-nic basket, and after a soul leaves a body.

BETH'S TOYS (CONT.)

Night-vision googly eye goggles:
For anyone who wants to stalk or peer into bedroom windows without losing a sense of childlike whimsy.

Sound-erasing sneakers:
Perfect for basketball players on the court, or football players trying to not wind up in court, these kicks are so fashionable, it's criminal.

False fingerprints:
Use a set of these handy stick-ons to easily and conveniently pass the blame onto someone else. Alibi not included.

Fall-asleep darts:
Deadlier than the darts found in any British pub, these beauties are perfectly weighted to immobilize anyone quicker than downing a keg. No gun needed!

Lie-detecting doll:
Some dolls blink, some dolls pee, but some dolls know when you're not telling the truth. And that doll will. Not. Like. It.

Indestructible baseball bat:
More durable than a professional baseball player's reputation, this bat is perfect for hitting balls, smashing vending machines, or intimidating the press to bury that police report.

Taser shaped like a ladybug:
As cute as a button, but more painful than getting your skin caught in a zipper, one zap will be enough to temporarily paralyze your victims and leave them seeing spots for days.

Fake police badge:
Claim jurisdiction and get into places that you aren't supposed to with ease.

Location-tracking stickers:
Available in puffy, scratch-and-sniff, and holographic, kids will love to trade these among themselves while you trade their locations with multinational corporations.

Rainbow-colored duct tape:
Why use regular duct-tape when you have some that has a little more pizazz? Prisoners will look fabulous when bound in this extra-long-lasting tape.

Mind-control hair clips:
When your friend's bangs are getting in the way of her doing your laundry, these fashionable accessories will kill two birds with one stone. They will also make her kill birds with stones if you wish.

Poison gum:
Double your pleasure with the extra-long-lasting flavor—and permanent death—found in the tasty sticks of bubblegum.

Pink sentient switchblade:
It's full of rage, ready to be your best friend, and is able to wait for years and years to start stabbing.

First Appearance: Season 3, Episode 9: "The ABC's of Beth"

*S**t, Rick. You made all of this stuff for my mom?*

The psychotic Apple doesn't fall far from the tree, you know.

Jeez, you won't even help me with my homework.

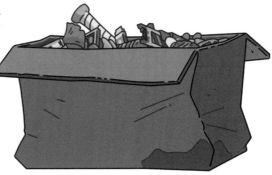

BLAST SHIELD WRISTWATCH

Rick has tons of enemies and since he never knows when it will be necessary to lower the blast shields, covering all of the doors and windows of the Smith homestead, it makes sense to keep a remote control on his wrist at all times. With the touch of a button, enemies are kept out (or in), while freedom (to stay or leave) is (or isn't) maintained.

First Appearance: Season 2, Episode 4: "Total Rickall"

button to ACTIVATE

Rick why does the house have blast shields.

Trust me, you don't WANNA KNOW how MANY ANSWERS that question has.

CITADEL OF RICKS

Founded by Ricks for the Freedom of Ricks, it is the secret headquarters of the Interdimensional Council of Ricks and a secured shelter for a few thousand other Ricks avoiding enemies such as galactic terrorists, subgalactic dictators, the Intergalactic Government, and more. It's nevertheless shunned by Rick (C-137), who believes that the point of being a Rick is being "a" Rick. Presided over by Ricks from other dimensions and with varying hairstyles and personalities, Rick (C-137) is recognized for his history of noncompliance and cooperation with the Council.

First Appearance: Season 1, Episode 10: "Close Rick-Counters of the Rick Kind"

I don't like it there, Morty. I can't abide bureaucracy—I don't like being told where to go or what to do. I consider it a violation.

FROOPYLAND

Though not Rick's best work, Froopyland still doesn't deserve to be s**t on creatively. Created for Beth, who remembered it only as an imaginary place, this child's wonderland was made by collapsing a quantum tesseract and filled with creatures made up of imaginary DNA.

Designed to be harmless, Froopyland had procedurally generated clouds, rivers made of rainbows, bouncy ground, and breathable water. It was also meant to keep Beth, and her slightly sociopathic tendencies, away from other people. Froopyland evolved, however, after Beth abandoned her childhood friend Tommy Lipnip there when she grew jealous of his stable home life. Left to his own devices, Tommy survived by mating with the Froopy creatures, creating Froopy–human hybrid

offspring and then consuming their cross-bred proteins.

First Appearance: Season 3, Episode 9: "The ABC's of Beth"

chalk opens
the portal

To live is to risk it all.
Otherwise you're just an inert chunk
of randomly assembled molecules drifting
wherever the universe blows you.

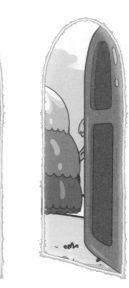

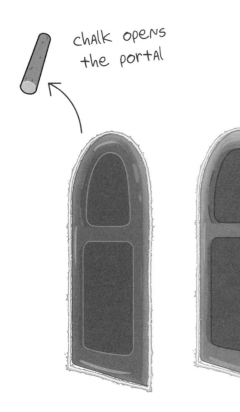

GRAPPLING SHOES

Comfortable enough to wear at home, but stylish and practical enough for the office or even the cliff you're working on, Rick's grappling shoes are the perfect accessories for any adventurer. Once you slap these on your feet, you'll be able to traverse any surface, be it horizontal, vertical, or anywhere in between. By eschewing fashionable red soles for ones that will keep you from dying, these grappling shoes are instantly customizable and offer a range of sizes from Super Genius to Challenged Pubescent. Just remember to turn them on and every jaunt will be a leisurely breeze.

First Appearance: Season 1, Episode 1: "Pilot"

Wear these babies and walk on any surface. Up. Down. Below. Turn around to the left, these bring it all together.

Yeah, these were pretty cool until I broke my legs.

Well, then someone should have turned them on.

HOLOGRAPHIC COSMOS PROJECTOR

Little more than one of those night-lights that projects a fake solar system in a kid's room—so they feel comfortable in their beds before really stopping to think about their place in the universe—this version uses advanced holographic technology and allows viewers an ultra-hi-definition view of the known universe. If you're smart enough to notice, it includes some of the unknown universe, too. It really impresses teenage girls.

First Appearance: Season 1, Episode 11: "Ricksy Business"

front view

Aww, man, that's a good idea.

If I were you, I wouldn't pull that thread.

JERRYBOREE

Located at 3924917, a totally unregistered cross-temporal asteroid, Jerryboree is a day care for Jerrys where they can romp and play, safely, with other Jerrys. Filled to the brim with activities such as golf, movie watching, a giant Beth mascot, and enough "funny" jokes that can be emailed from Jerry to Jerry for an eternity, its completely voluntary, open-door policy makes it the perfect place to leave a Jerry while on your adventure. Just remember to hold on to your claim ticket or you could be stuck with someone else's Jerry, which could be just as bad or worse.

First Appearance: Season 2, Episode 2: "Mortynight Run"

"Jerrys don't tend to last five minutes off of Earth. . . . Here they can romp and play with other Jerrys. It couldn't be safer."

—Rick

OVENLESS BROWNIES

It's incredible what a gifted mind can accomplish when priorities are in order. Those recipes you found online have nothing on Doofus Rick (or any of the Ricks), who knows that when you add titanium nitrate and a tad of chlorified tartrate, you get ovenless brownies. Chewy, chocolaty, and without any gritty or chemical aftertaste, you'll experience death by chocolate. Unless you experience death by Rick first.

First Appearance: Season 1, Episode 10: "Close Rick-Counters of the Rick Kind"

I wouldn't eat those. You know that Rick eats his own s***t right?

Ummm, oh geeez. That really shouldn't be in the book. Don't try that, that recipe. It'll kill you. Kill you dead.

PARTICLE BEAM WRISTWATCH

The particle beam wristwatch offers a pure clean death, not the snake-makery it appears to offer via slight-of-beam. Just point it at your victim, say something clever, hit the button, and poof—they're gone with only a snake left in their place. This watch might also be able to transmit and receive messages, create holo-clones, produce an energy shield, and fire laser beams, but that hasn't been proven yet.

First Appearance: Season 2, Episode 5: "Get Schwifty"

"Stay back! This watch turns people into snakes!"

—Rick

TIME GUN

The perfect weapon to murder yourself or your loved ones in current or other realities, the time gun can shoot across space and time to kill anyone in any timeline that has splintered from yours due to feeling uncertain. Of course, by killing yourself in one reality you exponentially diminish your ability, and the ability of you in other dimensions, to join back together. That's just a risk you have to take.

First Appearance: Season 2, Episode 1: "A Rickle in Time"

Rick Fact

It's probably easier to eliminate one of the possibilities rather than merge with them.

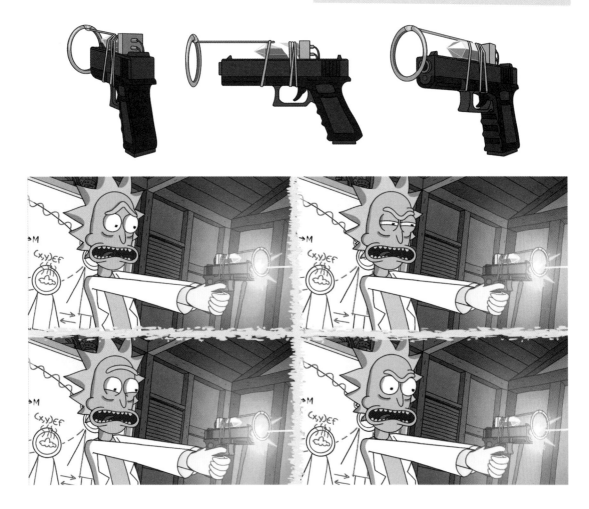

TIME PHONE

Constantly losing your phone, or yourself, in the existential miasma of this or other realities, and the "Find My Phone" or therapy apps aren't doing a good enough job? Walk passed the Genius Bar, to a bar with really good Wi-Fi and access to other dimensions, and try this simple life hack: insert a time crystal into your phone! As simple as that "press the spacebar to move the cursor all over the screen" thing, this easy add-on will allow you to call yourself in different realties.

Of course, procuring the highly protected time crystal itself will get you more time in a fourth-dimensional time prison than smuggling a Blood Diamond out of Africa would, it's totally worth the risk if for nothing more than activating the free roaming across dimensions. Your calls to yourself will immediately go to voice mail, though, because you're calling yourself, but since you'll be able to retrieve your voice mails yourself you'll be encouraging yourself all by yourself. And isn't that what the journey is all about?

First Appearance: Season 2, Episode 1: "A Rickle in Time"

TIME STABILIZING COLLAR

Time stabilizing collars can be synched up across realities and are particularly useful when wearers need to be brought back through time. Strong enough to traverse logic, they also have a tricky latch that you might have to tinker with in order to get it to close. They only work if the wearers are equally as decisive and the button on the collars are pressed at exactly the same time. So try a flat-head screwdriver. Maybe a Phillips-head.

First Appearance: Season 2, Episode 1: "A Rickle in Time"

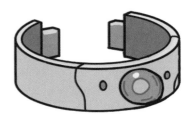

unlocked

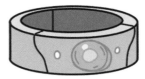

green = stablized

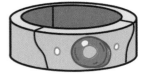

red = unstable

TRUE LEVEL

More precise than a bubble in a cheap hardware store level (which is a perfect representation of why the human species is a failure), true level is so beautiful it might completely ruin your life and send you spiraling headfirst into an emotional break. Created with a specialized power compactor, goggles, wooden mallet, and advanced digital leveling grid, this is a modern marvel and a masterpiece of engineering. Step into the perfectly level space and experience a near orgasmic sensation of being free from a world in which everything is crooked and reality is, in fact, poison.

First Appearance: Season 3, Episode 8: "Morty's Mind Blowers"

"Lambs to the cosmic slaughter!!"
—Morty

UNIVERSAL MAGNET

If you're looking for anything from a zip-tie to a date (or a date that's into zip-ties, if you know what I mean), there's nothing as attractive as a handheld universal magnet. Just type the name of whatever you're searching for into the keyboard base, power it up, and the universal magnet will draw dozens from within a 30-mile radius. Then, pick which one you want and leave the rest on the ground for someone else to pick up!

First Appearance: Season 3, Episode 8: "Morty's Mind Blowers"

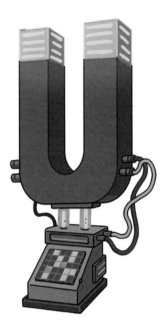

Rick Fact: Unity

A collective hive mind with a passion for unification, Unity traveled the universe to find herselves after breaking up with Rick. Unity took over a planet in order to become a Type 1 civilization so she could be invited into the Galactic Federation, which would lead to access to countless planets and species, which she could then unify, one by one, becoming the universe and, what the single-minded once called, a god.

WISHING PORTAL

There is a legend in the Citadel. A legend of a Wishing Portal. A portal where, if—and only if—a Morty threw something really important into it, his wish would be granted. Some think that the portal leads to a reality that is filled with french toast. Others believe it leads to a place with a bunch of flies everywhere. Some, though, dramatically think it leads nowhere. So if your wish is to be rid of your shameful tendencies, throw in a shell necklace and see what happens. If you wish for more sandwiches, try offering a panini maker.

But the truth is, wishes never come true. Not for Mortys. Not in the Citadel. Because the Wishing Portal is nothing more than a garbage dump. So you might as well throw yourself in.

First Appearance: Season 3, Episode 7: "The Ricklantis Mixup"

Rick Fact
XP20-XS is the most state-of-the-art prosthetic penis available in any reality.

INTERDIMENSIONAL GADGETS & SCIENCE

There are more things in Heaven and Earth, Horatio,
Than are dreamt of in your philosophy.

–*Hamlet* by William Shakespeare

There are more interdimensional things in this chapter, Reader,
Than were originally in the glossary.

–"Interdimensional Gadgets & Science" by Robb Pearlman

This chapter showcases all of the tech and gadgets that
originate from other dimensions because although Rick
C-137 is unquestionably the Rickest Rick of all Ricks, there
are other Ricks, and other scientists, in other dimensions
who, occasionally, come up with their own tech.

Oh s***t, guys, you're gonna burn out
the CPU with this one.

BRAINALYZER HELMET

If you've strapped someone into the Brainalyzer 9000, you're going to have to make sure you've upgraded to the helmet with a lightning cord because the Number Bugs in research and development did away with the round jack thing. What a money grab. It costs more and your other helmet is now basically worthless. Sure, the new Brainalyzer Helmet still interfaces with the Brainalyzer wires atop the crown to extract information and memories from the relaxed cerebellum of a subject, but the only thing truly different about this helmet is that it now includes optional racing stripes that run down the center of the darkened faceplate, and an automatic shut off once the subject's (victim's) brain is liquefied!

First Appearance: Season 3, Episode 1: "The Rickshank Rickdemption"

Brainalyzer 9000

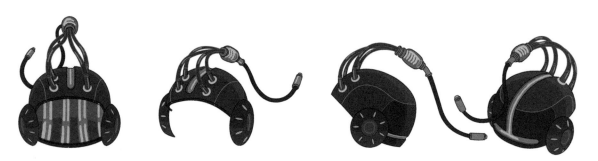

Brainalyzer Helmet

high tech gurney

high tech chair

BROKEN LEG SERUM

Found in a future where medical science has advanced to a stage where it takes longer to get a referral preapproved by your insurance company than it does to heal a bone (which is pretty much exactly how it is now, but with a lower co-pay, and fewer forms to fill out), the broken leg serum can be found in any corner pharmacy to heal mangled bones. If you or a loved one are helplessly writhing in abject agony, you'll be impressed with the speed with which those femurs, patellas, tibias, and fibulas are fused and straightened to their original forms.

First Appearance: Season 1, Episode 1: "Pilot"

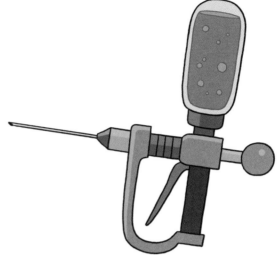

That stuff healed my broken legs, instantly. I've never felt so good in my life.

I guess, it is the little things, huh, Morty?

CONROY

Generously donated to every home by the Galactic Federation, Conroy the robot is a pill-dispensing, indispensable member of every human family. Shaped like an aerodynamic pear, Conroy's visual perception lenses are housed in a clear, helmetlike enclosure that keeps them dust-free under even the harshest of circumstances. Conroy's hands, located in the breastplate directly beneath the speaker hidden in his collar can extend, as do the hidden grappling arms located on his sides, to grab on to any object with just enough force to make it count.

Conroy moves not on wheels or treads, but via low-impact, rocket-powered levitation, which runs so silently you can clearly hear his authoritarian, British accent as he pours pills down your throat for breakfast, lunch, or dinner. More than a butler, more than a robot, he's your friend. Unless he sees you doing something the Galactic Government would disapprove of—in which case all the nice blue lights turn red, the easy floating cushion of air beneath him is replaced by four angry-looking, clawlike feet, and his voice turns from British mild to robot cop wild.

First Appearance: Season 3, Episode 1: "The Rickshank Rickdemption"

COURIER FLAPS

The intergalactic version of the muscly guy in the brown shirt and short shorts who delivers your packages, but less off-putting, the Courier Flaps are pink globs equipped with a camera and headset that deliver important packages across dimensions and planets. Birdperson uses Courier Flaps to deliver Eggvites—metallic, egg-shaped vessels that are used to invite people and birdpeople to annual events like parties or special events like weddings to underage, undercover Galactic Government operatives—but you can just use any old box.

First Appearance: Season 2, Episode 10: "The Wedding Squanchers"

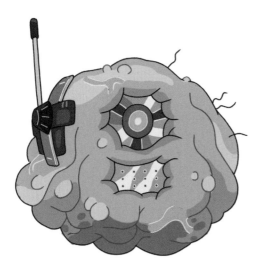

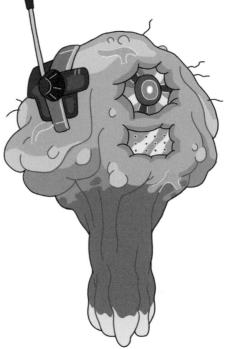

EVIL MORTY EYE-PATCH TRANSMITTER

Was Evil Rick truly evil? Probably, but he was probably made even more evil by Evil Morty, who controlled his Rick via a transmitter in his eye patch. Cleverly housed on the inside of what everyone believed to be a mere covering for an empty socket, the transmitter was, in fact, attached, via wires, through Evil Morty's eye and straight into his brain. Evil ideas were then transmitted via brain waves to a receiver implanted in Evil Rick's cranium.

Undetectable as a twist-ending nobody saw coming, this unique eye patch is a hot fashion statement and the perfect accessory for torturous schemes and assassinations.

First Appearance: Season 1, Episode 10: "Close Rick-Counters of the Rick Kind"

GWENDOLYN

A premiere creation of the Gazorpazorps, Gwendolyn is a humanoid sex robot featuring an open mouth, protruding frontal units, and a thong bikini. Far more advanced than the in-vitro fertilization methods, egg cryopreservation technology, or even artificial wombs used on Earth in most dimensions, Gwendolyn and her sister robots were specifically outfitted with genetic compilers and incubation chambers. Despite looking like overglorified, robotic sex dolls, they were created by the females of the Gazorpazopian race in order to continue their race without having to interact with their brutish male counterparts.

Like any invention designed to make life easier, like a slow cooker or vacuum cleaner, Gwendolyn's primary function is to save time as well as physical and emotional energy. Plus, by designing her and her sisters to appeal to the males' basest instincts, these robots are a win-win for everyone.

First Appearance: Season 1, Episode 7: "Raising Gazorpazorp"

front   side   back   bottom   top

Rick Fact

Though perfect for resonating through multiphases of quantum matter, this multiphase quantum resonator doesn't defraculate, so it's basically worthless. Try another pawnshop for one that works. But, if you can get it for 60 schmidgens, a fart, and a sex robot, take it.

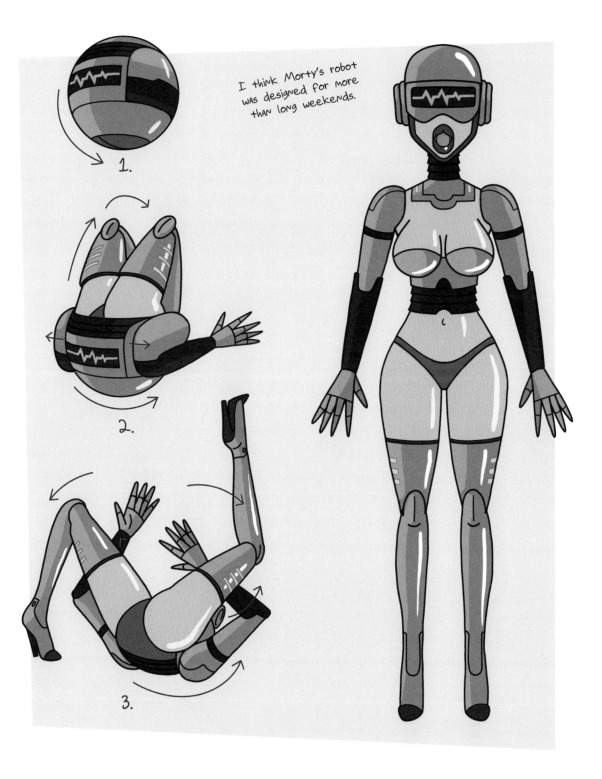

I think Morty's robot was designed for more than long weekends.

1.

2.

3.

IMMORTALITY FIELD

A protective force field that surrounds a resort planet, the immortality field allows travelers of all shapes and trunk numbers the kind of consequence-free vacation they're looking for. By emitting a web of microscopic theoretical time machines that can pinpoint and reverse the effects of any deathly adventure in real time, tourists from all dimensions can do what they want without the fear of death, disease, or dismemberment.

The planet also offers a variety of amusement park rides and attractions, including the Whirly Dirly, a roller coaster that, ever so briefly, leaves the immortality field. This is the perfect place to bring the most fragile being in the universe for some fun or any unsuspecting idiot in need of a simple explainable death. Five out of five stars.

First Appearance: Season 3, Episode 5: "The Whirly Dirly Conspiracy"

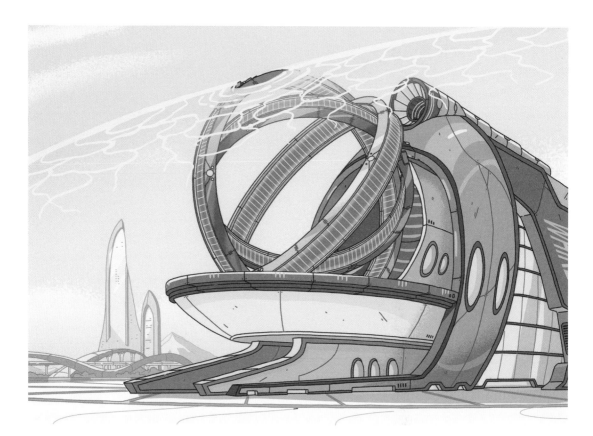

MEESEEKS BOX

In need of a friendly helper? Need a hand getting that chore done? Help is one button away. Push the blue button of a Meeseeks box and your very own Mr. Meeseeks will appear in a flash!

All you have to do is make a request of the eager-to-help blue humanoid with big black eyes and a tuft of red hair atop its balloon-like head, and they will fulfill your request and then happily stop existing. Don't worry, though, they're totally fine with going away once their purpose is fulfilled. Just be sure to keep your request simple, like getting popular or becoming a more fulfilled woman. They're not gods, they're Meeseeks, and the mounting frustration involved in trying to help you achieve your goal will undoubtedly cause chaos in the greater Meeseeks community.

First Appearance: Season 1, Episode 5: "Meeseeks and Destroy"

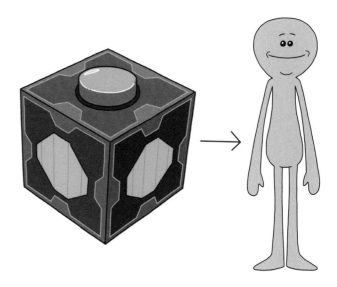

Rick Fact
The Fleeseeks Box is an apparatus for the containment of a mop and floor wax.

"I'm Mr. Meeseeks!
Look at me!"
—Mr. Meeseeks

PHOTOGRAPHY CYBORGS

An ace photographer that will never need to stop to replace film or flashbulbs, the photography cyborgs are adept at taking both staged and candid photos at any event or occasion. Perfect for weddings or bar mitzvahs, photography cyborgs have all the cameras and lenses implanted right in their heads. He's not staring at you, he's taking your picture, so take that look off your face and say cheese!

First Appearance: Season 2, Episode 10: "The Wedding Squanchers"

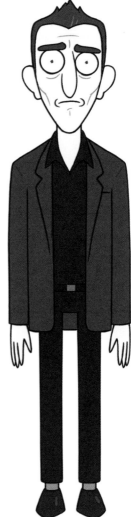

Rick Fact

When making a speech at a wedding, it's okay to write notes.
First, say hello. Then introduce yourself and how you know the groom or the bride. Then trail off. Then crumple up the note. Then ad-lib.

PLUMBUS

Everyone has a Plumbus in their home. First they take the dinglebop, and they smooth it out with a bunch of schleem. The schleem is then repurposed for later batches. They take the dinglebop and they push it through the grumbo, where the fleeb is rubed against it. It's important that the fleeb is rubbed because the fleeb has all of the fleeb juice. Then a schlami shows up, and he rubs it and spits on it. They cut the fleeb. There's several hizards in the way. The blamfs rub against the chumbles. And the ploobis and grumbo are shaved away. That leaves you with a regular, old Plumbus.

First Appearance: Season 2, Episode 8: "Interdimensional Cable 2: Tempting Fate"

ROY: A LIFE WELL LIVED

One of the, if not the most, popular games at Blips and Chitz, the multiple-world-famous interplanetary restaurant and amusement center where you can "Squirt, Squeeze, and Play All Day!" is Roy: A Life Well Lived. This virtual reality game invites players to inhabit the life of an everyman named Roy Parsons, from birth to death, and determine the kind of life he lives. From what to major in to who to marry and how to spend your vacations, every choice, even those relating to carpet and carpet-related careers, gain you points as you compete with others to be the best Roy you, and he, can be. Look out for the sequel, Roy 2: Dave, coming to a Blips and Chitz soon!

First Appearance: Season 2, Episode 2: "Mortynight Run"

"S--t! This guy's taking Roy off the grid! This guy doesn't have a Social Security number for Roy!"
—Blips and Chitz Patron

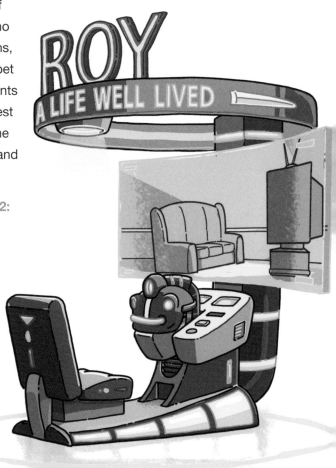

SYNTHETIC LASER EELS

Like the commonplace electric eels that served as energy sources for countless fan fiction horror and erotica stories, this mutated version of Electrophorus electricus has the ability to generate enough power to dissolve most matter, including but not limited to garage doors. They won't reach their full potential unless they're fully oxidized, which is a problem when keeping them in a garage and not an accredited laboratory or aquarium.

First Appearance: Season 1, Episode 11: "Ricksy Business"

SLOW MOBIUS'S CLOCK STAFFS

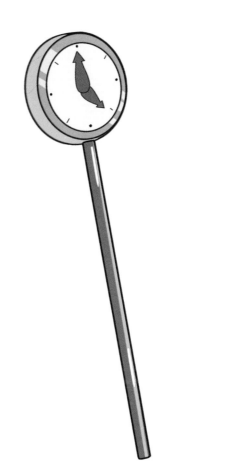

If you're a fan of scenes from 1980s movies in which the girl of the hero's dreams walks into a room in slow motion, and also a fan of unexpected humor, then you must insist Slow Mobius bring his clock staffs to your next party. Imbued with the ability to slow time via concentrated beams of warped space time, Slow Mobius can target any booty shake or hair toss you think worthy of a long, lingering second or even tenth look. Measuring about six feet tall, and only usable as a pair, they're a pain to travel with, but worth the trouble for the laughs.

First Appearance: Season 1, Episode 11: "Ricksy Business"

THERAPY HELMET

One of the primary tools used to aid in marital disputes and utilized by the counselors on Nuptia 4, this therapy helmet renders artificial, biological representations of couples' perceptions of each other, also known as mythologues. These thought-forms are constructs created when a husband or wife wears the helmet and thinks of his or her partner and are harmless if contained, but deadly if codependent and freed from their holding cells. There are no regrets allowed in counseling, so if you think your S.O. is a S.O.B., the mythologues will fight it out for you.

First Appearance: Season 2, Episode 7: "Big Trouble in Little Sanchez"

Too bad we didn't get tickets to that fight.

Aww, come on, Rick. Those are my parents.

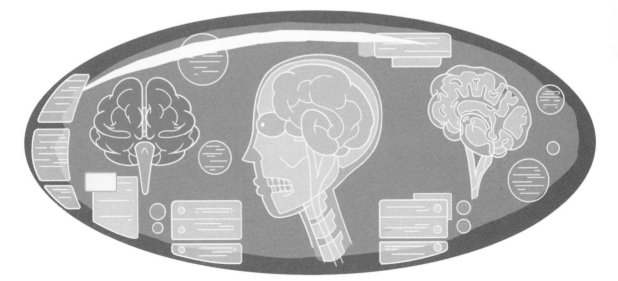

brain scanner

TIME CRYSTAL

Stolen from omniscient immortal testicle monsters with the ability to transcend time and space, time crystals can be added to: a gun, a phone, or a time stabilizing device to transcend realities. Also known as crystallized Anthenite, time crystals are illegal to obtain in most, if not all, dimensions and if found with one in your possession you could be looking at a life sentence in Time Prison.

First Appearance: Season 2, Episode 1: "A Rickle in Time"

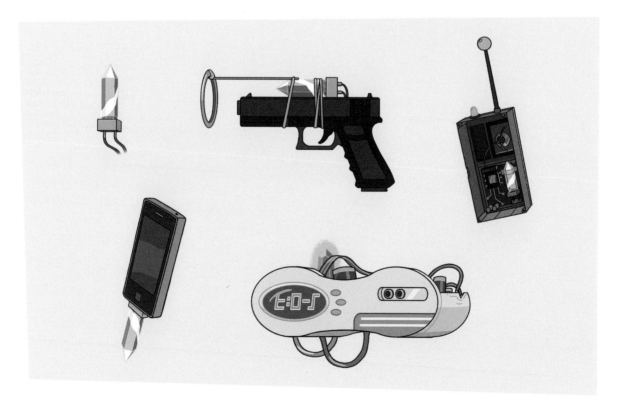

VINDIBEACON

Gifted to Rick and Morty after their first adventure with The Vindicators, the super team of Morty's heroes who are first line of defense against evil, the Vindibeacon is designed for them to literally answer a call to adventure. An amethyst colored crystal housed on top of a base with a speaker and microphone port, it is wirelessly and trans-dimensionally connected to the CPU of the Vindicators base of operations. Used only when the universe itself is at stake, the Vindibeacon lights up and emits a pleasant, come-hither tone, calling the Vindicator diaspora to assemble.

First Appearance: Season 3, Episode 4: "Vindicators 3: The Return of the Worldender"

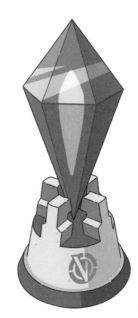

ZIGERION SIMULATION CHAMBER

Housed on a containment pad on a Zigerion spaceship, everything you see in the simulation chamber is made up of nanobotic renderings generated by crystalline chips held in the ship's CPU unit. Created by the galaxy's most ambitious, least successful con-artists—who are really uncomfortable with nudity—the simulation chamber's sole purpose is to extract information from abducted humans and other sentient life forms by making them think they were in familiar surroundings and lulling them into a sense of false comfort.

Unfortunately, Zigerion technology is glitchy, and their knowledge of other cultures is limited, so their simulations are imperfect. If you're paying attention you might see a pastry who lives in a toaster drive off to work in a smaller toaster with wheels or, even more unlikely, a satisfied wife post-coital. Zigerions are crafty, so watch out for their simulation within a simulation within a simulation trick. But, let's be honest, only a complete idiot would fall for that. *You've got a point there.*

First Appearance: Season 1, Episode 4: "M. Night Shaym-Aliens!"

"So what if the most meaningful day of your life was just a simulation running at minimal capacity?"
—Rick

THANKS & ACKNOWLEDGMENTS

I'd like to thank everyone at Adult Swim and Running Press, especially Britny Brooks and Cindy De La Hoz-Sipala for the opportunity, and their patience. Special thanks must be scooped like so much ice cream upon *Rick and Morty* creators Justin Roiland and Dan Harmon for giving this reality a look at what others may offer. Thanks also to David and Oscar for their patience as I dove headfirst into any and all portals. And last, but certainly not least, I have to thank my very best friend in the world, Mr. Poopy Butthole, who's been by my side for as long as I can remember. You're the man, Mr. Poopy Butthole!